AUCTeX 11.88 Reference Manual

A catalogue record for this book is available from the Hong Kong Public Libraries.

Published in Hong Kong by Samurai Media Limited.

Email: info@samuraimedia.org

ISBN 978-988-8381-51-7

Background Cover Image by https://www.flickr.com/people/webtreatsetc/

Table of Contents

Appendix A   Copying, Changes, Development, FAQ, Texinfo Mode 80

Indices 106

Executive Summary

AUCTEX is an integrated environment for editing LaTeX, ConTEXt, docTEX, Texinfo, and TEX files.

Although AUCTEX contains a large number of features, there are no reasons to despair. You can continue to write TEX and LaTeX documents the way you are used to, and only start using the multiple features in small steps. AUCTEX is not monolithic, each feature described in this manual is useful by itself, but together they provide an environment where you will make very few LaTeX errors, and makes it easy to find the errors that may slip through anyway.

It is a good idea to make a printout of AUCTEX's reference card `tex-ref.tex` or one of its typeset versions.

If you want to make AUCTEX aware of style files and multi-file documents right away, insert the following in your `.emacs` file.

```
(setq TeX-auto-save t)
(setq TeX-parse-self t)
(setq-default TeX-master nil)
```

Another thing you should enable is RefTEX, a comprehensive solution for managing cross references, bibliographies, indices, document navigation and a few other things. (see Section "Installation" in *The RefTEX manual*)

For detailed information about the **preview-latex** subsystem of AUCTEX, see Section "Introduction" in *The* **preview-latex** *Manual*.

There is a mailing list for general discussion about AUCTEX: write a mail with "subscribe" in the subject to `auctex-request@gnu.org` to join it. Send contributions to `auctex@gnu.org`.

Bug reports should go to `bug-auctex@gnu.org`, suggestions for new features, and pleas for help should go to either `auctex-devel@gnu.org` (the AUCTEX developers), or to `auctex@gnu.org` if they might have general interest. Please use the command *M-x TeX-submit-bug-report RET* to report bugs if possible. You can subscribe to a low-volume announcement list by sending "subscribe" in the subject of a mail to `info-auctex-request@gnu.org`.

Copying

AUCTeX primarily consists of Lisp files for Emacs (and XEmacs), but there are also installation scripts and files and TeX support files. All of those are *free*; this means that everyone is free to use them and free to redistribute them on a free basis. The files of AUCTeX are not in the public domain; they are copyrighted and there are restrictions on their distribution, but these restrictions are designed to permit everything that a good cooperating citizen would want to do. What is not allowed is to try to prevent others from further sharing any version of these programs that they might get from you.

Specifically, we want to make sure that you have the right to give away copies of the files that constitute AUCTeX, that you receive source code or else can get it if you want it, that you can change these files or use pieces of them in new free programs, and that you know you can do these things.

To make sure that everyone has such rights, we have to forbid you to deprive anyone else of these rights. For example, if you distribute copies of parts of AUCTeX, you must give the recipients all the rights that you have. You must make sure that they, too, receive or can get the source code. And you must tell them their rights.

Also, for our own protection, we must make certain that everyone finds out that there is no warranty for AUCTeX. If any parts are modified by someone else and passed on, we want their recipients to know that what they have is not what we distributed, so that any problems introduced by others will not reflect on our reputation.

The precise conditions of the licenses for the files currently being distributed as part of AUCTeX are found in the General Public Licenses that accompany them. This manual specifically is covered by the GNU Free Documentation License (see Section A.1 [Copying this Manual], page 80).

1 Introduction

1.1 Overview of AUCTEX

AUCTEX is a comprehensive customizable integrated environment for writing input files for TEX, LATEX, ConTEXt, Texinfo, and docTEX using Emacs or XEmacs.

It supports you in the insertion of macros, environments, and sectioning commands by providing completion alternatives and prompting for parameters. It automatically indents your text as you type it and lets you format a whole file at once. The outlining and folding facilities provide you with a focused and clean view of your text.

AUCTEX lets you process your source files by running TEX and related tools (such as output filters, post processors for generating indices and bibliographies, and viewers) from inside Emacs. AUCTEX lets you browse through the errors TEX reported, while it moves the cursor directly to the reported error, and displays some documentation for that particular error. This will even work when the document is spread over several files.

One component of AUCTEX that LATEX users will find attractive is preview-latex, a combination of folding and in-source previewing that provides true "What You See Is What You Get" experience in your sourcebuffer, while letting you retain full control.

More detailed information about the features and usage of AUCTEX can be found in the remainder of this manual.

AUCTEX is written entirely in Emacs Lisp, and hence you can easily add new features for your own needs. It is a GNU project and distributed under the 'GNU General Public License Version 3'.

The most recent version is always available at `http://ftp.gnu.org/pub/gnu/auctex/`.

WWW users may want to check out the AUCTEX page at `http://www.gnu.org/software/auctex/`.

For comprehensive information about how to install AUCTEX See Section 1.2 [Installation], page 3, or Section 1.2.7 [Installation under MS Windows], page 10, respectively.

If you are considering upgrading AUCTEX, the recent changes are described in Section A.2 [Changes], page 87.

If you want to discuss AUCTEX with other users or its developers, there are several mailing lists you can use.

Send a mail with the subject "subscribe" to `auctex-request@gnu.org` in order to join the general discussion list for AUCTEX. Articles should be sent to `auctex@gnu.org`. In a similar way, you can subscribe to the `info-auctex@gnu.org` list for just getting important announcements about AUCTEX. The list `bug-auctex@gnu.org` is for bug reports which you should usually file with the *M-x TeX-submit-bug-report RET* command. If you want to address the developers of AUCTEX themselves with technical issues, they can be found on the discussion list `auctex-devel@gnu.org`.

1.2 Installing AUCTEX

The simplest way of installing AUCTEX is by using the Emacs package manager integrated in Emacs 24 and greater (ELPA). Simply do *M-x package-list-packages RET*, mark the auctex package for installation with *i*, and hit *x* to execute the installation procedure. That's all.

The remainder of this section is about installing AUCTEX from a release tarball or from a checkout of the AUCTEX repository.

Installing AUCTEX should be simple: merely `./configure`, `make`, and `make install` for a standard site-wide installation (most other installations can be done by specifying a `--prefix=...` option).

On many systems, this will already activate the package, making its modes the default instead of the built-in modes of Emacs. If this is not the case, consult Section 1.2.4 [Loading the package], page 7. Please read through this document fully before installing anything. The installation procedure has changed as compared to earlier versions. Users of MS Windows are asked to consult See Section 1.2.7 [Installation under MS Windows], page 10.

1.2.1 Prerequisites

- A recent version of Emacs, alternatively XEmacs

  Emacs 20 is no longer supported, and neither is XEmacs with a version of `xemacs-base` older than 1.84 (released in sumo from 02/02/2004). Using preview-latex requires a version of Emacs compiled with image support. While the X11 version of Emacs 21 will likely work, Emacs 22 and later is preferred.

  Windows   Precompiled versions are available from `ftp://ftp.gnu.org/gnu/emacs/windows/`.

  Mac OS X For an overview of precompiled versions of Emacs for Mac OS X see for example `http://www.emacswiki.org/cgi-bin/wiki/EmacsForMacOS`.

  GNU/Linux

   Most GNU/Linux distributions nowadays provide a recent variant of Emacs via their package repositories.

  Self-compiled

   Compiling Emacs yourself requires a C compiler and a number of tools and development libraries. Details are beyond the scope of this manual. Instructions for checking out the source code can be found at `https://savannah.gnu.org/bzr/?group=emacs`.

  If you really need to use Emacs 21 on platforms where this implies missing image support, you should disable the installation of preview-latex (see below).

  While XEmacs (version 21.4.15, 21.4.17 or later) is supported, doing this in a satisfactory manner has proven to be difficult. This is mostly due to technical shortcomings and differing API's which are hard to come by. If AUCTEX is your main application for XEmacs, you are likely to get better results and support by switching to Emacs. Of course, you can improve support for your favorite editor by giving feedback in case you encounter bugs.

- A working TEX installation

  Well, AUCTEX would be pointless without that. Processing documentation requires TEX, LATEX and Texinfo during installation. preview-latex requires Dvips for its operation in DVI mode. The default configuration of AUCTEX is tailored for teTEX or TEXlive-based distributions, but can be adapted easily.

- A recent Ghostscript

  This is needed for operation of preview-latex in both DVI and PDF mode. Most versions of Ghostscript nowadays in use should work fine (version 7.0 and newer).

- The texinfo package

  Strictly speaking, you can get away without it if you are building from the distribution tarball, have not modified any files and don't need a printed version of the manual: the pregenerated info file is included in the tarball. At least version 4.0 is required.

For some known issues with various software, see Section "Known problems" in *the* preview-latex *manual*.

1.2.2 Configure

The first step is to configure the source code, telling it where various files will be. To do so, run

```
./configure options
```

(Note: if you have fetched AUCTEX from Git rather than a regular release, you will have to first follow the instructions in README.GIT).

On many machines, you will not need to specify any options, but if configure cannot determine something on its own, you'll need to help it out with one of these options:

--prefix=/usr/local

All automatic placements for package components will be chosen from sensible existing hierarchies below this: directories like man, share and bin are supposed to be directly below *prefix*.

Only if no workable placement can be found there, in some cases an alternative search will be made in a prefix deduced from a suitable binary.

/usr/local is the default *prefix*, intended to be suitable for a site-wide installation. If you are packaging this as an operating system component for distribution, the setting /usr will probably be the right choice. If you are planning to install the package as a single non-priviledged user, you will typically set *prefix* to your home directory.

--with-emacs[=/path/to/emacs]

If you are using a pretest which isn't in your $PATH, or configure is not finding the right Emacs executable, you can specify it with this option.

--with-xemacs[=/path/to/xemacs]

Configure for generation under XEmacs (Emacs is the default). Again, the name of the right XEmacs executable can be specified, complete with path if necessary.

--with-packagedir=/dir

This XEmacs-only option configures the directory for XEmacs packages. A typical user-local setting would be ~/.xemacs/xemacs-packages. If this directory exists and is below *prefix*, it should be detected automatically. This will install and activate the package.

`--without-packagedir`

>   This XEmacs-only option switches the detection of a package directory and
>   corresponding installation off. Consequently, the Emacs installation scheme
>   will be used. This might be appropriate if you are using a different package
>   system/installer than the XEmacs one and want to avoid conflicts.
>
>   The Emacs installation scheme has the following options:

`--with-lispdir=`*/dir*

>   This Emacs-only option specifies the location of the `site-lisp` directory within
>   'load-path' under which the files will get installed (the bulk will get installed
>   in a subdirectory). `./configure` should figure this out by itself.

`--with-auctexstartfile=auctex.el`
`--with-previewstartfile=preview-latex.el`

>   This is the name of the respective startup files. If *lispdir* contains a subdirectory
>   `site-start.d`, the start files are placed there, and `site-start.el` should load
>   them automatically. Please be aware that you must not move the start files
>   after installation since other files are found *relative* to them.

`--with-packagelispdir=auctex`

>   This is the directory where the bulk of the package gets located. The startfile
>   adds this into *load-path*.

`--with-auto-dir=`*/dir*

>   You can use this option to specify the directory containing automatically gen-
>   erated information. It is not necessary for most TeX installs, but may be used
>   if you don't like the directory that configure is suggesting.

`--help`   This is not an option specific to AUCTeX. A number of standard options to
>   `configure` exist, and we do not have the room to describe them here; a short
>   description of each is available, using `--help`. If you use '`--help=recursive`',
>   then also **preview-latex**-specific options will get listed.

`--disable-preview`

>   This disables configuration and installation of **preview-latex**. This option is not
>   actually recommended. If your Emacs does not support images, you should
>   really upgrade to a newer version. Distributors should, if possible, refrain from
>   distributing AUCTeX and **preview-latex** separately in order to avoid confusion
>   and upgrade hassles if users install partial packages on their own.

`--with-texmf-dir=`*/dir*
`--without-texmf-dir`

>   This option is used for specifying a TDS-compliant directory hierarchy. Using
>   `--with-texmf-dir=`*/dir* you can specify where the TeX TDS directory hierar-
>   chy resides, and the TeX files will get installed in */dir*`/tex/latex/preview/`.
>
>   If you use the `--without-texmf-dir` option, the TeX-related files will be kept
>   in the Emacs Lisp tree, and at runtime the `TEXINPUTS` environment variable
>   will be made to point there. You can install those files into your own TeX tree
>   at some later time with *M-x preview-install-styles RET*.

`--with-tex-dir=/dir`

> If you want to specify an exact directory for the preview TeX files, use `--with-tex-dir=/dir`. In this case, the files will be placed in */dir*, and you'll also need the following option:

`--with-doc-dir=/dir`

> This option may be used to specify where the TeX documentation goes. It is to be used when you are using `--with-tex-dir=/dir`, but is normally not necessary otherwise.

1.2.3 Build/install

Once `configure` has been run, simply enter

        make

at the prompt to byte-compile the lisp files, extract the TeX files and build the documentation files. To install the files into the locations chosen earlier, type

        make install

You may need special privileges to install, e.g., if you are installing into system directories.

1.2.4 Loading the package

You can detect the successful activation of AUCTeX and preview-latex in the menus after loading a LaTeX file like `preview/circ.tex`: AUCTeX then gives you a 'Command' menu, and preview-latex gives you a 'Preview' menu.

For XEmacs, if the installation occured into a valid package directory (which is the default), then this should work out of the box.

With Emacs (or if you explicitly disabled use of the package system), the startup files `auctex.el` and `preview-latex.el` may already be in a directory of the `site-start.d/` variety if your Emacs installation provides it. In that case they should be automatically loaded on startup and nothing else needs to be done. If not, they should at least have been placed somewhere in your `load-path`. You can then load them by placing the lines

        (load "auctex.el" nil t t)
        (load "preview-latex.el" nil t t)

into your init file.

If you explicitly used `--with-lispdir`, you may need to add the specified directory into Emacs' `load-path` variable by adding something like

        (add-to-list 'load-path "~/elisp")

before the above lines into your Emacs startup file.

For site-wide activation in GNU Emacs, see See Section 1.2.5 [Advice for package providers], page 8.

Once activated, the modes provided by AUCTeX are used per default for all supported file types. If you want to change the modes for which it is operative instead of the default, use

        M-x customize-variable RET TeX-modes RET

If you want to remove a preinstalled AUCTeX completely before any of its modes have been used,

```
(unload-feature 'tex-site)
```
should accomplish that.

1.2.5 Providing AUCTeX as a package

As a package provider, you should make sure that your users will be served best according to their intentions, and keep in mind that a system might be used by more than one user, with different preferences.

There are people that prefer the built-in Emacs modes for editing TeX files, in particular plain TeX users. There are various ways to tell AUCTeX even after auto-activation that it should not get used, and they are described in Chapter 1 [Introduction to AUCTeX], page 3.

So if you have users that don't want to use the preinstalled AUCTeX, they can easily get rid of it. Activating AUCTeX by default is therefore a good choice.

If the installation procedure did not achieve this already by placing `auctex.el` and `preview-latex.el` into a possibly existing `site-start.d` directory, you can do this by placing

```
(load "auctex.el" nil t t)
(load "preview-latex.el" nil t t)
```
in the system-wide `site-start.el`.

If your package is intended as an XEmacs package or to accompany a precompiled version of Emacs, you might not know which TeX system will be available when `preview-latex` gets used. In this case you should build using the `--without-texmf-dir` option described previously. This can also be convenient for systems that are intended to support more than a single TeX distribution. Since more often than not TeX packages for operating system distributions are either much more outdated or much less complete than separately provided systems like TeX Live, this method may be generally preferable when providing packages.

The following package structure would be adequate for a typical fully supported Unix-like installation:

'preview-tetex'
> Style files and documentation for `preview.sty`, placed into a TeX tree where it is accessible from the teTeX executables usually delivered with a system. If there are other commonly used TeX system packages, it might be appropriate to provide separate packages for those.

'auctex-emacs-tetex'
> This package will require the installation of 'preview-tetex' and will record in 'TeX-macro-global' where to find the TeX tree. It is also a good idea to run
>
> > `emacs -batch -f TeX-auto-generate-global`
>
> when either AUCTeX or teTeX get installed or upgraded. If your users might want to work with a different TeX distribution (nowadays pretty common), instead consider the following:

'auctex-emacs'
> This package will be compiled with '`--without-texmf-dir`' and will consequently contain the '`preview`' style files in its private directory. It will probably not be possible to initialize 'TeX-macro-global' to a sensible value, so

running 'TeX-auto-generate-global' does not appear useful. This package would neither conflict with nor provide 'preview-tetex'.

'auctex-xemacs-tetex'
'auctex-xemacs'

Those are the obvious XEmacs equivalents. For XEmacs, there is the additional problem that the XEmacs sumo package tree already possibly provides its own version of AUCTeX, and the user might even have used the XEmacs package manager to updating this package, or even installing a private AUCTeX version. So you should make sure that such a package will not conflict with existing XEmacs packages and will be at an appropriate place in the load order (after site-wide and user-specific locations, but before a distribution-specific sumo package tree). Using the --without-packagedir option might be one idea to avoid conflicts. Another might be to refrain from providing an XEmacs package and just rely on the user or system administrator to instead use the XEmacs package system.

1.2.6 Installation for non-privileged users

Often people without system administration privileges want to install software for their private use. In that case you need to pass more options to the configure script. For XEmacs users, this is fairly easy, because the XEmacs package system has been designed to make this sort of thing practical: but GNU Emacs users (and XEmacs users for whom the package system is for some reason misbehaving) may need to do a little more work.

The main expedient is using the --prefix option to the configure script, and let it point to the personal home directory. In that way, resulting binaries will be installed under the bin subdirectory of your home directory, manual pages under man and so on. It is reasonably easy to maintain a bunch of personal software, since the prefix argument is supported by most configure scripts.

You'll have to add something like /home/myself/share/emacs/site-lisp to your load-path variable, if it isn't there already.

XEmacs users can achieve the same end by pointing configure at an appropriate package directory (normally --with-packagedir=~/.xemacs/xemacs-packages will serve). The package directory stands a good chance at being detected automatically as long as it is in a subtree of the specified *prefix*.

Now here is another thing to ponder: perhaps you want to make it easy for other users to share parts of your personal Emacs configuration. In general, you can do this by writing '~myself/' anywhere where you specify paths to something installed in your personal subdirectories, not merely '~/', since the latter, when used by other users, will point to non-existent files.

For yourself, it will do to manipulate environment variables in your .profile resp. .login files. But if people will be copying just Elisp files, their copies will not work. While it would in general be preferable if the added components where available from a shell level, too (like when you call the standalone info reader, or try using preview.sty for functionality besides of Emacs previews), it will be a big help already if things work from inside of Emacs.

Here is how to do the various parts:

Making the Elisp available

In GNU Emacs, it should be sufficient if people just do

```
(load "~myself/share/emacs/site-lisp/auctex.el" nil t t)
(load "~myself/share/emacs/site-lisp/preview-latex.el" nil t t)
```

where the path points to your personal installation. The rest of the package should be found relative from there without further ado.

In XEmacs, you should ask the other users to add symbolic links in the subdirectories `lisp`, `info` and `etc` of their `~/.xemacs/xemacs-packages/` directory. (Alas, there is presently no easy programmatic way to do this, except to have a script do the symlinking for them.)

Making the Info files available

For making the info files accessible from within Elisp, something like the following might be convenient to add into your or other people's startup files:

```
(eval-after-load 'info
   '(add-to-list 'Info-directory-list "~myself/info"))
```

In XEmacs, as long as XEmacs can see the package, there should be no need to do anything at all; the info files should be immediately visible. However, you might want to set `INFOPATH` anyway, for the sake of standalone readers outside of XEmacs. (The info files in XEmacs are normally in `~/.xemacs/xemacs-packages/info`.)

Making the LaTeX style available

If you want others to be able to share your installation, you should configure it using '`--without-texmf-dir`', in which case things should work as well for them as for you.

1.2.7 Installation under MS Windows

In a Nutshell

The following are brief installation instructions for the impatient. In case you don't understand some of this, run into trouble of some sort, or need more elaborate information, refer to the detailed instructions further below.

1. Install the prerequisites, i.e. Emacs or XEmacs, MSYS or Cygwin, a TeX system, and Ghostscript.

2. Open the MSYS shell or a Cygwin shell and change to the directory containing the unzipped file contents.

3. Configure AUCTeX:

   For Emacs: Many people like to install AUCTeX into the pseudo file system hierarchy set up by the Emacs installation. Assuming Emacs is installed in `C:/Program Files/Emacs` and the directory for local additions of your TeX system, e.g. MiKTeX, is `C:/localtexmf`, you can do this by typing the following statement at the shell prompt:

   ```
   ./configure --prefix='C:/Program Files/Emacs' \
     --infodir='C:/Program Files/Emacs/info' \
     --with-texmf-dir='C:/localtexmf'
   ```

For XEmacs: You can install AUCTEX as an XEmacs package. Assuming XEmacs is installed in `C:/Program Files/XEmacs` and the directory for local additions of your TEX system, e.g. MiKTEX, is `C:/localtexmf`, you can do this by typing the following command at the shell prompt:

```
./configure --with-xemacs='C:/Program Files/XEmacs/bin/xemacs' \
    --with-texmf-dir='C:/localtexmf'
```

The commands above are examples for common usage. More on configuration options can be found in the detailed installation instructions below.

If the configuration script failed to find all required programs, make sure that these programs are in your system path and add directories containing the programs to the `PATH` environment variable if necessary. Here is how to do that in W2000/XP:

1. On the desktop, right click "My Computer" and select properties.
2. Click on "Advanced" in the "System Properties" window.
3. Select "Environment Variables".
4. Select "path" in "System Variables" and click "edit". Move to the front in the line (this might require scrolling) and add the missing path including drive letter, ended with a semicolon.

4. If there were no further error messages, type

```
make
```

In case there were, please refer to the detailed description below.

5. Finish the installation by typing

```
make install
```

Detailed Installation Instructions

Installation of AUCTEX under Windows is in itself not more complicated than on other platforms. However, meeting the prerequisites might require more work than on some other platforms, and feel less natural.

If you are experiencing any problems, even if you think they are of your own making, be sure to report them to `auctex-devel@gnu.org` so that we can explain things better in future.

Windows is a problematic platform for installation scripts. The main problem is that the installation procedure requires consistent file names in order to find its way in the directory hierarchy, and Windows path names are a mess.

The installation procedure tries finding stuff in system search paths and in Emacs paths. For that to succeed, you have to use the same syntax and spelling and case of paths everywhere: in your system search paths, in Emacs' `load-path` variable, as argument to the scripts. If your path names contain spaces or other 'shell-unfriendly' characters, most notably backslashes for directory separators, place the whole path in '`"double quote marks"`' whenever you specify it on a command line.

Avoid 'helpful' magic file names like '`/cygdrive/c`' and '`C:\PROGRA~1\`' like the plague. It is quite unlikely that the scripts will be able to identify the actual file names involved. Use the full paths, making use of normal Windows drive letters like ' '`C:/Program Files/Emacs`' ' where required, and using the same combination of upper- and lowercase letters as in the actual files. File names containing shell-special characters like spaces or backslashes (if you prefer that syntax) need to get properly quoted to the shell: the above example used single quotes for that.

Ok, now here are the steps to perform:

1. You need to unpack the AUCTEX distribution (which you seemingly have done since you are reading this). It must be unpacked in a separate installation directory outside of your Emacs file hierarchy: the installation will later copy all necessary files to their final destination, and you can ultimately remove the directory where you unpacked the files.

   Line endings are a problem under Windows. The distribution contains only text files, and theoretically most of the involved tools should get along with that. However, the files are processed by various utilities, and it is conceivable that not all of them will use the same line ending conventions. If you encounter problems, it might help if you try unpacking (or checking out) the files in binary mode, if your tools allow that.

   If you don't have a suitable unpacking tool, skip to the next step: this should provide you with a working 'unzip' command.

2. The installation of AUCTEX will require the MSYS tool set from `http://www.mingw.org/` or the Cygwin tool set from `http://cygwin.com/`. The latter is slower and larger (the download size of the base system is about 15 MB) but comes with a package manager that allows for updating the tool set and installing additional packages like, for example, the spell checker aspell.

   If Cygwin specific paths like '/cygdrive/c' crop up in the course of the installation, using a non-Cygwin Emacs could conceivably cause trouble. Using Cygwin either for everything or nothing might save headaches, *if* things don't work out.

3. Install a current version of XEmacs from `http://www.xemacs.org/` or Emacs from `ftp://ftp.gnu.org/gnu/emacs/windows/`. Emacs is the recommended choice because it is currently the primary platform for AUCTEX development.

4. You need a working TEX installation. One popular installation under Windows is MiKTEX (`http://www.miktex.org`). Another much more extensive system is TEX Live (`http://www.tug.org/texlive`) which is rather close to its Unix cousins.

5. A working copy of Ghostscript (`http://www.cs.wisc.edu/~ghost/`) is required for preview-latex operation. Examining the output from

       gswin32c -h

   on a Windows command line should tell you whether your Ghostscript supports the png16m device needed for PNG support. MiKTEX apparently comes with its own Ghostscript called 'mgs.exe'.

6. Perl (`http://www.perl.org`) is needed for rebuilding the documentation if you are working with a copy from Git or have touched documentation source files in the preview-latex part. If the line endings of the file preview/latex/preview.dtx don't correspond with what Perl calls \n when reading text files, you'll run into trouble.

7. Now the fun stuff starts. If you have not yet done so, unpack the AUCTEX distribution into a separate directory after rereading the instructions for unpacking above.

8. Ready for takeoff. Start some shell (typically bash) capable of running configure, change into the installation directory and call ./configure with appropriate options.

Typical options you'll want to specify will be

`--prefix=`*drive:/path/to/emacs-hierarchy*

> which tells `configure` where to perform the installation. It may also make `configure` find Emacs or XEmacs automatically; if this doesn't happen, try one of '`--with-emacs`' or '`--with-xemacs`' as described below. All automatic detection of files and directories restricts itself to directories below the *prefix* or in the same hierarchy as the program accessing the files. Usually, directories like `man`, `share` and `bin` will be situated right under *prefix*.
>
> This option also affects the defaults for placing the Texinfo documentation files (see also '`--infodir`' below) and automatically generated style hooks.
>
> If you have a central directory hierarchy (not untypical with Cygwin) for such stuff, you might want to specify its root here. You stand a good chance that this will be the only option you need to supply, as long as your TeX-related executables are in your system path, which they better be for AUCTeX's operation, anyway.

`--with-emacs`

> if you are installing for a version of Emacs. You can use '`--with-emacs=`*drive:/path/to/emacs*' to specify the name of the installed Emacs executable, complete with its path if necessary (if Emacs is not within a directory specified in your `PATH` environment setting).

`--with-xemacs`

> if you are installing for a version of XEmacs. Again, you can use '`--with-xemacs=`*drive:/path/to/xemacs*' to specify the name of the installed XEmacs executable complete with its path if necessary. It may also be necessary to specify this option if a copy of Emacs is found in your `PATH` environment setting, but you still would like to install a copy of AUCTeX for XEmacs.

`--with-packagedir=`*drive:/dir*

> is an XEmacs-only option giving the location of the package directory. This will install and activate the package. Emacs uses a different installation scheme:

`--with-lispdir=`*drive:/path/to/site-lisp*

> This Emacs-only option tells a place in `load-path` below which the files are situated. The startup files `auctex.el` and `preview-latex.el` will get installed here unless a subdirectory `site-start.d` exists which will then be used instead. The other files from AUCTeX will be installed in a subdirectory called `auctex`.
>
> If you think that you need a different setup, please refer to the full installation instructions in Section 1.2.2 [Configure], page 5.

`--infodir=`*drive:/path/to/info/directory*

> If you are installing into an Emacs directory, info files have to be put into the `info` folder below that directory. The configuration script will usually try to install into the folder `share/info`, so you have to override this by

specifying something like '`--infodir='C:/Program Files/info`'' for the configure call.

`--with-auto-dir=`*drive:/dir*

Directory containing automatically generated information. You should not normally need to set this, as '`--prefix`' should take care of this.

`--disable-preview`

Use this option if your Emacs version is unable to support image display. This will be the case if you are using a native variant of Emacs 21.

`--with-texmf-dir=`*drive:/dir*

This will specify the directory where your TeX installation sits. If your TeX installation does not conform to the TDS (TeX directory standard), you may need to specify more options to get everything in place.

For more information about any of the above and additional options, see Section 1.2.2 [Configure], page 5.

Calling `./configure --help=recursive` will tell about other options, but those are almost never required.

Some executables might not be found in your path. That is not a good idea, but you can get around by specifying environment variables to `configure`:

```
GS="drive:/path/to/gswin32c.exe" ./configure ...
```

should work for this purpose. `gswin32c.exe` is the usual name for the required *command line* executable under Windows; in contrast, `gswin32.exe` is likely to fail.

As an alternative to specifying variables for the `configure` call you can add directories containing the required executables to the `PATH` variable of your Windows system. This is especially a good idea if Emacs has trouble finding the respective programs later during normal operation.

9. Run `make` in the installation directory.

10. Run `make install` in the installation directory.

11. With XEmacs, AUCTeX and preview-latex should now be active by default. With Emacs, activation depends on a working `site-start.d` directory or similar setup, since then the startup files `auctex.el` and `preview-latex.el` will have been placed there. If this has not been done, you should be able to load the startup files manually with

```
(load "auctex.el" nil t t)
(load "preview-latex.el" nil t t)
```

in either a site-wide `site-start.el` or your personal startup file (usually accessible as `~/.emacs` from within Emacs and `~/.xemacs/init.el` from within XEmacs).

The default configuration of AUCTeX is probably not the best fit for Windows systems with MiKTeX. You might want to add

```
(require 'tex-mik)
```

after loading `auctex.el` and `preview-latex.el` in order to get more appropriate values for some customization options.

You can always use

> *M-x customize-group RET AUCTeX RET*

in order to customize more stuff, or use the 'Customize' menu.

12. Load `preview/circ.tex` into Emacs or XEmacs and see if you get the 'Command' menu. Try using it to LATEX the file.

13. Check whether the 'Preview' menu is available in this file. Use it to generate previews for the document.

    If this barfs and tells you that image type 'png' is not supported, you can either add PNG support to your Emacs installation or choose another image format to be used by preview-latex.

    Adding support for an image format usually involves the installation of a library, e.g. from `http://gnuwin32.sf.net/`. If you got your Emacs from `gnu.org` you might want to check its README file (`ftp://ftp.gnu.org/gnu/emacs/windows/README`) for details.

    A different image format can be chosen by setting the variable `preview-image-type`. While it is recommended to keep the 'dvipng' or 'png' setting, you can temporarily select a different format like 'pnm' to check if the lack of PNG support is the only problem with your Emacs installation.

    Try adding the line

    ```
    (setq preview-image-type 'pnm)
    ```

    to your init file for a quick test. You should remove the line after the test again, because PNM files take away **vast** amounts of disk space, and thus also of load/save time.

    Well, that about is all. Have fun!

1.2.8 Customizing

Most of the site-specific customization should already have happened during configuration of AUCTEX. Any further customization can be done with customization buffers directly in Emacs. Just type *M-x customize-group RET AUCTeX RET* to open the customization group for AUCTEX or use the menu entries provided in the mode menus. Editing the file `tex-site.el` as suggested in former versions of AUCTEX should not be done anymore because the installation routine will overwrite those changes.

You might check some variables with a special significance. They are accessible directly by typing *M-x customize-variable RET <variable> RET*.

TeX-macro-global   [User Option]
    Directories containing the site's TEX style files.

Normally, AUCTEX will only allow you to complete macros and environments which are built-in, specified in AUCTEX style files or defined by yourself. If you issue the *M-x TeX-auto-generate-global* command after loading AUCTEX, you will be able to complete on all macros available in the standard style files used by your document. To do this, you must set this variable to a list of directories where the standard style files are located. The directories will be searched recursively, so there is no reason to list subdirectories explicitly. Automatic configuration will already have set the variable for you if it could use the program 'kpsewhich'. In this case you normally don't have to alter anything.

1.3 Quick Start

AUCTEX is a powerful program offering many features and configuration options. If you are new to AUCTEX this might be deterrent. Fortunately you do not have to learn everything at once. This Quick Start Guide will give you the knowledge of the most important commands and enable you to prepare your first LaTeX document with AUCTEX after only a few minutes of reading.

In this introduction, we assume that AUCTEX is already installed on your system. If this is not the case, you should read the file INSTALL in the base directory of the unpacked distribution tarball. These installation instructions are available in this manual as well, Section 1.2 [Installation], page 3. We also assume that you are familiar with the way keystrokes are written in Emacs manuals. If not, have a look at the Emacs Tutorial in the Help menu.

If AUCTEX is installed, you might still need to activate it, by inserting

```
(load "auctex.el" nil t t)
```

in your user init file.[1] If you've installed AUCTEX from the Emacs package manager (ELPA), you must not have this line in your user init file. The installation procedure already cares about loading AUCTEX correctly.

In order to get support for many of the LaTeX packages you will use in your documents, you should enable document parsing as well, which can be achieved by putting

```
(setq TeX-auto-save t)
(setq TeX-parse-self t)
```

into your init file. Finally, if you often use \include or \input, you should make AUCTEX aware of the multi-file document structure. You can do this by inserting

```
(setq-default TeX-master nil)
```

into your init file. Each time you open a new file, AUCTEX will then ask you for a master file.

This Quick Start Guide covers two main topics: First we explain how AUCTEX helps you in editing your input file for TeX, LaTeX, and some other formats. Then we describe the functions that AUCTEX provides for processing the input files with LaTeX, BibTeX, etc., and for viewing and debugging.

1.3.1 Functions for editing TeX files

1.3.1.1 Making your TeX code more readable

AUCTEX can do syntax highlighting of your source code, that means commands will get special colors or fonts. You can enable it locally by typing *M-x font-lock-mode RET*. If you want to have font locking activated generally, enable **global-font-lock-mode**, e.g. with *M-x customize-variable RET global-font-lock-mode RET*.

AUCTEX will indent new lines to indicate their syntactical relationship to the surrounding text. For example, the text of a \footnote or text inside of an environment will be indented relative to the text around it. If the indenting has gotten wrong after adding or

---

[1] This usually is a file in your home directory called .emacs if you are utilizing GNU Emacs or .xemacs/init.el if you are using XEmacs.

deleting some characters, use TAB to reindent the line, *M-q* for the whole paragraph, or *M-x LaTeX-fill-buffer RET* for the whole buffer.

1.3.1.2 Entering sectioning commands

Insertion of sectioning macros, that is '\chapter', '\section', '\subsection', etc. and accompanying '\label' commands may be eased by using *C-c C-s*. You will be asked for the section level. As nearly everywhere in AUCTₑX, you can use the TAB or SPC key to get a list of available level names, and to auto-complete what you started typing. Next, you will be asked for the printed title of the section, and last you will be asked for a label to be associated with the section.

1.3.1.3 Inserting environments

Similarly, you can insert environments, that is '\begin{}'–'\end{}' pairs: Type *C-c C-e*, and select an environment type. Again, you can use TAB or SPC to get a list, and to complete what you type. Actually, the list will not only provide standard LᴬTₑX environments, but also take your '\documentclass' and '\usepackage' commands into account if you have parsing enabled by setting TeX-parse-self to t. If you use a couple of environments frequently, you can use the up and down arrow keys (or *M-p* and *M-n*) in the minibuffer to get back to the previously inserted commands.

Some environments need additional arguments. Often, AUCTₑX knows about this and asks you to enter a value.

1.3.1.4 Inserting macros

C-c C-m, or simply *C-c RET* will give you a prompt that asks you for a LᴬTₑX macro. You can use TAB for completion, or the up/down arrow keys (or *M-p* and *M-n*) to browse the command history. In many cases, AUCTₑX knows which arguments a macro needs and will ask you for that. It even can differentiate between mandatory and optional arguments—for details, see Section 2.6 [Completion], page 31.

An additional help for inserting macros is provided by the possibility to complete macros right in the buffer. With point at the end of a partially written macro, you can complete it by typing *M-TAB*.

1.3.1.5 Changing the font

AUCTₑX provides convenient keyboard shortcuts for inserting macros which specify the font to be used for typesetting certain parts of the text. They start with *C-c C-f*, and the last *C-* combination tells AUCTₑX which font you want:

C-c C-f C-b
> Insert **bold face** '\textbf{⋆}' text.

C-c C-f C-i
> Insert *italics* '\textit{⋆}' text.

C-c C-f C-e
> Insert *emphasized* '\emph{⋆}' text.

C-c C-f C-s
> Insert *slanted* '\textsl{⋆}' text.

`C-c C-f C-r`
> Insert roman \textrm{⋆} text.

`C-c C-f C-f`
> Insert sans serif '\textsf{⋆}' text.

`C-c C-f C-t`
> Insert typewriter '\texttt{⋆}' text.

`C-c C-f C-c`
> Insert SMALL CAPS '\textsc{⋆}' text.

`C-c C-f C-d`
> Delete the innermost font specification containing point.

If you want to change font attributes of existing text, mark it as a region, and then invoke the commands. If no region is selected, the command will be inserted with empty braces, and you can start typing the changed text.

Most of those commands will also work in math mode, but then macros like **\mathbf** will be inserted.

1.3.1.6 Other useful features

AUCTEX also tries to help you when inserting the right "quote" signs for your language, dollar signs to typeset math, or pairs of braces. It offers shortcuts for commenting out text (`C-c ;` for the current region or `C-c %` for the paragraph you are in). The same keystrokes will remove the % signs, if the region or paragraph is commented out yet. With **TeX-fold-mode**, you can hide certain parts (like footnotes, references etc.) that you do not edit currently. Support for Emacs' outline mode is provided as well. And there's more, but this is beyond the scope of this Quick Start Guide.

1.3.2 Creating and viewing output, debugging

1.3.2.1 One Command for LaTeX, helpers, viewers, and printing

If you have typed some text and want to run LaTeX (or TeX, or other programs—see below) on it, type `C-c C-c`. If applicable, you will be asked whether you want to save changes, and which program you want to invoke. In many cases, the choice that AUCTEX suggests will be just what you want: first **latex**, then a viewer. If a **latex** run produces or changes input files for **makeindex**, the next suggestion will be to run that program, and AUCTEX knows that you need to run **latex** again afterwards—the same holds for BibTEX.

When no processor invocation is necessary anymore, AUCTEX will suggest to run a viewer, or you can chose to create a PostScript file using **dvips**, or to directly print it.

At this place, a warning needs to be given: First, although AUCTEX is really good in detecting the standard situations when an additional **latex** run is necessary, it cannot detect it always. Second, the creation of PostScript files or direct printing currently only works when your output file is a DVI file, not a PDF file.

Ah, you didn't know you can do both? That brings us to the next topic.

1.3.2.2 Choosing an output format

From a LATEX file, you can produce DVI output, or a PDF file directly *via* `pdflatex`. You can switch on source specials for easier navigation in the output file, or tell `latex` to stop after an error (usually `\noninteractive` is used, to allow you to detect all errors in a single run).

These options are controlled by toggles, the keystrokes should be easy to memorize:

`C-c C-t C-p`
>> This command toggles between DVI and PDF output

`C-c C-t C-i`
>> toggles interactive mode

`C-c C-t C-s`
>> toggles source specials support

`C-c C-t C-o`
>> toggles usage of Omega/lambda.

1.3.2.3 Debugging LATEX

When AUCTEX runs a program, it creates an output buffer in which it displays the output of the command. If there is a syntactical error in your file, `latex` will not complete successfully. AUCTEX will tell you that, and you can get to the place where the first error occured by pressing `C-c '` (the last character is a backtick). The view will be split in two windows, the output will be displayed in the lower buffer, and both buffers will be centered around the place where the error ocurred. You can then try to fix it in the document buffer, and use the same keystrokes to get to the next error. This procedure may be repeated until all errors have been dealt with. By pressing `C-c C-w` (`TeX-toggle-debug-boxes`) you can toggle whether AUCTEX should notify you of overfull and underfull boxes in addition to regular errors.

If a command got stuck in a seemingly infinite loop, or you want to stop execution for other reasons, you can use `C-c C-k` (for "kill"). Similar to `C-l`, which centers the buffer you are in around your current position, `C-c C-l` centers the output buffer so that the last lines added at the bottom become visible.

1.3.2.4 Running LATEX on parts of your document

If you want to check how some part of your text looks like, and do not want to wait until the whole document has been typeset, then mark it as a region and use `C-c C-r`. It behaves just like `C-c C-c`, but it only uses the document preamble and the region you marked.

If you are using `\include` or `\input` to structure your document, try `C-c C-b` while you are editing one of the included files. It will run `latex` only on the current buffer, using the preamble from the master file.

2 Editing the Document Source

The most commonly used commands/macros of AUCTEX are those which simply insert templates for often used TEX, LATEX, or ConTEXt constructs, like font changes, handling of environments, etc. These features are very simple, and easy to learn, and help you avoid mistakes like mismatched braces, or '\begin{}'-'\end{}' pairs.

Apart from that this chapter contains a description of some features for entering more specialized sorts of text, for formatting the source by indenting and filling and for navigating through the document.

2.1 Insertion of Quotes, Dollars, and Braces

Quotation Marks

In TEX, literal double quotes '"like this"' are seldom used, instead two single quotes are used '``like this''. To help you insert these efficiently, AUCTEX allows you to continue to press " to insert two single quotes. To get a literal double quote, press " twice.

TeX-insert-quote *count*   [Command]
> (") Insert the appropriate quote marks for TEX.
>
> Inserts the value of **TeX-open-quote** (normally '``') or **TeX-close-quote** (normally '''') depending on the context. With prefix argument, always inserts '"' characters.

TeX-open-quote   [User Option]
> String inserted by typing " to open a quotation. (See Section 5.4.1 [European], page 64, for language-specific quotation mark insertion.)

TeX-close-quote   [User Option]
> String inserted by typing " to close a quotation. (See Section 5.4.1 [European], page 64, for language-specific quotation mark insertion.)

TeX-quote-after-quote   [User Option]
> Determines the behavior of ". If it is non-nil, typing " will insert a literal double quote. The respective values of **TeX-open-quote** and **TeX-close-quote** will be inserted after typing " once again.

The 'babel' package provides special support for the requirements of typesetting quotation marks in many different languages. If you use this package, either directly or by loading a language-specific style file, you should also use the special commands for quote insertion instead of the standard quotes shown above. AUCTEX is able to recognize several of these languages and will change quote insertion accordingly. See Section 5.4.1 [European], page 64, for details about this feature and how to control it.

In case you are using the 'csquotes' package, you should customize LaTeX-csquotes-open-quote, LaTeX-csquotes-close-quote and LaTeX-csquotes-quote-after-quote. The quotation characters will only be used if both variables—LaTeX-csquotes-open-quote and LaTeX-csquotes-close-quote—are non-empty strings. But then the 'csquotes'-related values will take precedence over the language-specific ones.

Dollar Signs

In AUCTEX, dollar signs should match like they do in TEX. This has been partially implemented, we assume dollar signs always match within a paragraph. By default, the first '$' you insert in a paragraph will do nothing special. The second '$' will match the first. This will be indicated by moving the cursor temporarily over the first dollar sign.

TeX-insert-dollar *arg*   [Command]

    (*$*) Insert dollar sign.

    Show matching dollar sign if this dollar sign end the TEX math mode.

    With optional *arg*, insert that many dollar signs.

TEX and LATEX users often look for a way to insert inline equations like '$...$' or '\(...\)' simply typing *$*. AUCTEX helps them through the customizable variable **TeX-electric-math**.

TeX-electric-math   [User Option]

    If the variable is non-nil and you type *$* outside math mode, AUCTEX will automatically insert the opening and closing symbols for an inline equation and put the point between them. The opening symbol will blink when **blink-matching-paren** is non-nil. If **TeX-electric-math** is nil, typing *$* simply inserts '$' at point, this is the default.

    Besides **nil**, possible values for this variable are (**cons "$" "$"**) for TEX inline equations '$...$', and (**cons "\\(" "\\)"**) for LATEX inline equations '\(...\)'.

    If the variable is non-nil and point is inside math mode right between a couple of single dollars, pressing *$* will insert another pair of dollar signs and leave the point between them. Thus, if **TeX-electric-math** is set to (**cons "$" "$"**) you can easily obtain a TEX display equation '$$...$$' by pressing *$* twice in a row. (Note that you should not use double dollar signs in LATEX because this practice can lead to wrong spacing in typeset documents.)

    In addition, when the variable is non-nil and there is an active region outside math mode, typing *$* will put around the active region symbols for opening and closing inline equation and keep the region active, leaving point after the closing symbol. By pressing repeatedly *$* while the region is active you can toggle between an inline equation, a display equation, and no equation. To be precise, '$...$' is replaced by '$$...$$', whereas '\(...\)' is replaced by '\[...\]'.

If you want to automatically insert '$...$' in plain TEX files, and '\(...\)' in LATEX files by pressing *$*, add the following to your init file

```
(add-hook 'plain-TeX-mode-hook
  (lambda () (set (make-variable-buffer-local 'TeX-electric-math)
  (cons "$" "$"))))
(add-hook 'LaTeX-mode-hook
  (lambda () (set (make-variable-buffer-local 'TeX-electric-math)
  (cons "\\(" "\\)"))))
```

Braces

To avoid unbalanced braces, it is useful to insert them pairwise. You can do this by typing `C-c {`.

TeX-insert-braces [Command]

> (`C-c {`) Make a pair of braces and position the cursor to type inside of them. If there is an active region, put braces around it and leave point after the closing brace.

When writing complex math formulas in LaTeX documents, you sometimes need to adjust the size of braces with pairs of macros like '`\left`'-'`\right`', '`\bigl`'-'`\bigr`' and so on. You can avoid unbalanced pairs with the help of **TeX-insert-macro**, bound to `C-c C-m` or `C-c RET` (see Section 2.6 [Completion], page 31). If you insert left size adjusting macros such as '`\left`', '`\bigl`' etc. with **TeX-insert-macro**, it asks for left brace to use and supplies automatically right size adjusting macros such as '`\right`', '`\bigr`' etc. and corresponding right brace in addtion to the intended left macro and left brace.

The completion by **TeX-insert-macro** also applies when entering macros such as '`\langle`', '`\lfloor`' and '`\lceil`', which produce the left part of the paired braces. For example, inserting '`\lfloor`' by `C-c C-m` is immediately followed by the insertion of '`\rfloor`'. In addition, if the point was located just after '`\left`' or its friends, the corresponding '`\right`' etc. will be inserted in front of '`\rfloor`'. In both cases, active region is honored.

As a side effect, when **LaTeX-math-mode** (see Section 2.5 [Mathematics], page 30) is on, just typing '`(`' inserts not only '`\langle`', but also '`\rangle`'.

If you do not like such auto completion at all, it can be disabled by a user option.

TeX-arg-right-insert-p [User Option]

> If this option is turned off, the automatic supply of the right macros and braces is suppressed.

When you edit LaTeX documents, you can enable automatic brace pairing when typing `(`, `{` and `[`.

LaTeX-electric-left-right-brace [User Option]

> If this option is on, just typing `(`, `{` or `[` immediately adds the corresponding right brace ')', '}' or ']'. The point is left after the opening brace. If there is an active region, braces are put around it.

> They recognize the preceeding backslash or size adjusting macros such as '`\left`', '`\bigl`' etc., so the following completions will occur:
> - (when typing single left brace)
>   - '`(`' -> '`()`'
>   - '`{`' -> '`{}`'
>   - '`[`' -> '`[]`'
> - (when typing left brace just after a backslash)
>   - '`\(`' -> '`\(\)`'
>   - '`\{`' -> '`\{\}`'
>   - '`\[`' -> '`\[\]`'

- (when typing just after '\left' or '\bigl')
  - '\left(' -> '\left(\right)'
  - '\bigl[' -> '\bigl[\bigr]'
- (when typing just after '\Bigl\')
  - '\Bigl\{' -> '\Bigl\{\Bigr\}'

This auto completion feature may be a bit annoying when editing an already existing LaTeX document. In that case, use *C-u 1* or *C-q* before typing (, { or [. Then no completion is done and just a single left brace is inserted. In fact, with optional prefix *arg*, just that many open braces are inserted without any completion.

2.2 Inserting Font Specifiers

Perhaps the most used keyboard commands of AUCTeX are the short-cuts available for easy insertion of font changing macros.

If you give an argument (that is, type *C-u*) to the font command, the innermost font will be replaced, i.e. the font in the TeX group around point will be changed. The following table shows the available commands, with ⋆ indicating the position where the text will be inserted.

C-c C-f C-b
> Insert **bold face** '\textbf{⋆}' text.

C-c C-f C-i
> Insert *italics* '\textit{⋆}' text.

C-c C-f C-e
> Insert *emphasized* '\emph{⋆}' text.

C-c C-f C-s
> Insert *slanted* '\textsl{⋆}' text.

C-c C-f C-r
> Insert roman \textrm{⋆} text.

C-c C-f C-f
> Insert sans serif '\textsf{⋆}' text.

C-c C-f C-t
> Insert typewriter '\texttt{⋆}' text.

C-c C-f C-c
> Insert SMALL CAPS '\textsc{⋆}' text.

C-c C-f C-d
> Delete the innermost font specification containing point.

TeX-font *replace what*   [Command]
> (*C-c C-f*) Insert template for font change command.

> If *replace* is not nil, replace current font. *what* determines the font to use, as specified by TeX-font-list.

`TeX-font-list`   [User Option]

>   List of fonts used by `TeX-font`.
>
>   Each entry is a list with three elements. The first element is the key to activate the font. The second element is the string to insert before point, and the third element is the string to insert after point. An optional fourth element means always replace if not nil.

`LaTeX-font-list`   [User Option]

>   List of fonts used by `TeX-font` in LaTeX mode. It has the same structure as `TeX-font-list`.

2.3 Inserting chapters, sections, etc.

Insertion of sectioning macros, that is '`\chapter`', '`\section`', '`\subsection`', etc. and accompanying '`\label`''s may be eased by using *C-c C-s*. This command is highly customizable, the following describes the default behavior.

When invoking you will be asked for a section macro to insert. An appropriate default is automatically selected by AUCTeX, that is either: at the top of the document; the top level sectioning for that document style, and any other place: The same as the last occurring sectioning command.

Next, you will be asked for the actual name of that section, and last you will be asked for a label to be associated with that section. The label will be prefixed by the value specified in `LaTeX-section-hook`.

`LaTeX-section` *arg*   [Command]

>   (*C-c C-s*) Insert a sectioning command.
>
>   Determine the type of section to be inserted, by the argument *arg*.
>
>   - If *arg* is nil or missing, use the current level.
>   - If *arg* is a list (selected by C-u), go downward one level.
>   - If *arg* is negative, go up that many levels.
>   - If *arg* is positive or zero, use absolute level:
>   + 0 : part
>   + 1 : chapter
>   + 2 : section
>   + 3 : subsection
>   + 4 : subsubsection
>   + 5 : paragraph
>   + 6 : subparagraph
>
>   The following variables can be set to customize the function.
>
>   `LaTeX-section-hook`
>
>   >   Hooks to be run when inserting a section.
>
>   `LaTeX-section-label`
>
>   >   Prefix to all section references.

The precise behavior of `LaTeX-section` is defined by the contents of `LaTeX-section-hook`.

`LaTeX-section-hook`   [User Option]

List of hooks to run when a new section is inserted.

The following variables are set before the hooks are run

level   Numeric section level, default set by prefix arg to `LaTeX-section`.

name   Name of the sectioning command, derived from *level*.

title   The title of the section, default to an empty string.

toc   Entry for the table of contents list, default nil.

done-mark

Position of point afterwards, default nil meaning after the inserted text.

A number of hooks are already defined. Most likely, you will be able to get the desired functionality by choosing from these hooks.

`LaTeX-section-heading`

Query the user about the name of the sectioning command. Modifies *level* and *name*.

`LaTeX-section-title`

Query the user about the title of the section. Modifies *title*.

`LaTeX-section-toc`

Query the user for the toc entry. Modifies *toc*.

`LaTeX-section-section`

Insert LATEX section command according to *name*, *title*, and *toc*. If *toc* is nil, no toc entry is inserted. If *toc* or *title* are empty strings, *done-mark* will be placed at the point they should be inserted.

`LaTeX-section-label`

Insert a label after the section command. Controlled by the variable `LaTeX-section-label`.

To get a full featured `LaTeX-section` command, insert

```
(setq LaTeX-section-hook
      '(LaTeX-section-heading
  LaTeX-section-title
  LaTeX-section-toc
  LaTeX-section-section
  LaTeX-section-label))
```

in your `.emacs` file.

The behavior of `LaTeX-section-label` is determined by the variable `LaTeX-section-label`.

LaTeX-section-label   [User Option]

 Default prefix when asking for a label.

 If it is a string, it is used unchanged for all kinds of sections. If it is nil, no label is inserted. If it is a list, the list is searched for a member whose car is equal to the name of the sectioning command being inserted. The cdr is then used as the prefix. If the name is not found, or if the cdr is nil, no label is inserted.

 By default, chapters have a prefix of 'cha:' while sections and subsections have a prefix of 'sec:'. Labels are not automatically inserted for other types of sections.

2.4 Inserting Environment Templates

A large apparatus is available that supports insertions of environments, that is '\begin{}' — '\end{}' pairs.

AUCTEX is aware of most of the actual environments available in a specific document. This is achieved by examining your '\documentclass' command, and consulting a precompiled list of environments available in a large number of styles.

Most of these are described further in the following sections, and you may easily specify more. See Section 2.4.5 [Customizing Environments], page 29.

You insert an environment with *C-c C-e*, and select an environment type. Depending on the environment, AUCTEX may ask more questions about the optional parts of the selected environment type. With *C-u C-c C-e* you will change the current environment.

LaTeX-environment *arg*   [Command]

 (*C-c C-e*) AUCTEX will prompt you for an environment to insert. At this prompt, you may press TAB or SPC to complete a partially written name, and/or to get a list of available environments. After selection of a specific environment AUCTEX may prompt you for further specifications.

 If the optional argument *arg* is not-nil (i.e. you have given a prefix argument), the current environment is modified and no new environment is inserted.

AUCTEX helps you adding labels to environments which use them, such as 'equation', 'figure', 'table', etc... When you insert one of the supported environments with *C-c C-e*, you will be automatically prompted for a label. You can select the prefix to be used for such environments with the **LaTeX-label-alist** variable.

LaTeX-label-alist   [User Option]

 List the prefixes to be used for the label of each supported environment.

 This is an alist whose car is the environment name, and the cdr either the prefix or a symbol referring to one.

 If the name is not found, or if the cdr is nil, no label is automatically inserted for that environment.

 If you want to automatically insert a label for a environment but with an empty prefix, use the empty string "" as the cdr of the corresponding entry.

As a default selection, AUCTEX will suggest the environment last inserted or, as the first choice the value of the variable **LaTeX-default-environment**.

LaTeX-default-environment   [User Option]

> Default environment to insert when invoking 'LaTeX-environment' first time. When
> the current environment is 'document', it is overriden by **LaTeX-default-document-environment**.

LaTeX-default-document-environment   [Variable]

> Default environment when invoking 'LaTeX-environment' and the current environ-
> ment is 'document'. It is intended to be used in LaTeX class style files. For example,
> in `beamer.el` it is set to `frame`, in `letter.el` to `letter`, and in `slides.el` to `slide`.

If the document is empty, or the cursor is placed at the top of the document,
AUCTeX will default to insert a 'document' environment prompting also for the insertion
of '\documentclass' and '\usepackage' macros. You will be prompted for a new package
until you enter nothing. If you do not want to insert any '\usepackage' at all, just press
RET at the first 'Packages' prompt.

AUCTeX distinguishes normal and expert environments. By default, it will offer completion only for normal environments. This behavior is controlled by the user option
TeX-complete-expert-commands.

TeX-complete-expert-commands   [User Option]

> Complete macros and environments marked as expert commands.
>
> Possible values are nil, t, or a list of style names.
>
> nil   Don't complete expert commands (default).
>
> t   Always complete expert commands.
>
> (STYLES ...)
> > Only complete expert commands of STYLES.

You can close the current environment with *C-c]*, but we suggest that you use *C-c C-e*
to insert complete environments instead.

LaTeX-close-environment   [Command]

> (*C-c]*) Insert an '\end' that matches the current environment.

AUCTeX offers keyboard shortcuts for moving point to the beginning and to the end of
the current environment.

LaTeX-find-matching-begin   [Command]

> (*C-M-a*) Move point to the '\begin' of the current environment.
>
> If this command is called inside a comment and **LaTeX-syntactic-comments** is en-
> abled, try to find the environment in commented regions with the same comment
> prefix.

LaTeX-find-matching-end   [Command]

> (*C-M-e*) Move point to the '\end' of the current environment.
>
> If this command is called inside a comment and **LaTeX-syntactic-comments** is en-
> abled, try to find the environment in commented regions with the same comment
> prefix.

2.4.1 Equations

When inserting equation-like environments, the '\label' will have a default prefix, which is controlled by the following variables:

LaTeX-equation-label   [User Option]
> Prefix to use for 'equation' labels.

LaTeX-eqnarray-label   [User Option]
> Prefix to use for 'eqnarray' labels.

LaTeX-amsmath-label   [User Option]
> Prefix to use for amsmath equation labels. Amsmath equations include 'align', 'alignat', 'xalignat', 'aligned', 'flalign' and 'gather'.

2.4.2 Floats

Figures and tables (i.e., floats) may also be inserted using AUCTEX. After choosing either 'figure' or 'table' in the environment list described above, you will be prompted for a number of additional things.

float position
> This is the optional argument of float environments that controls how they are placed in the final document. In LaTeX this is a sequence of the letters 'htbp' as described in the LaTeX manual. The value will default to the value of `LaTeX-float`.

caption
> This is the caption of the float. The default is to insert the caption at the bottom of the float. You can specify floats where the caption should be placed at the top with `LaTeX-top-caption-list`.

label
> The label of this float. The label will have a default prefix, which is controlled by the variables `LaTeX-figure-label` and `LaTeX-table-label`.

Moreover, you will be asked if you want the contents of the float environment to be horizontally centered. Upon a positive answer a '\centering' macro will be inserted at the beginning of the float environment.

LaTeX-float   [User Option]
> Default placement for floats.

LaTeX-figure-label   [User Option]
> Prefix to use for figure labels.

LaTeX-table-label   [User Option]
> Prefix to use for table labels.

LaTeX-top-caption-list   [User Option]
> List of float environments with top caption.

2.4.3 Itemize-like Environments

In an itemize-like environment, nodes (i.e., '\item's) may be inserted using *C-c LFD*.

LaTeX-insert-item   [Command]
> (*C-c LFD*) Close the current item, move to the next line and insert an appropriate
> '\item' for the current environment. That is, 'itemize' and 'enumerate' will have
> '\item ' inserted, while 'description' will have '\item[]' inserted.

TeX-arg-item-label-p   [User Option]
> If non-nil, you will always be asked for optional label in items. Otherwise, you will
> be asked only in description environments.

2.4.4 Tabular-like Environments

When inserting Tabular-like environments, that is, 'tabular' 'array' etc., you will be
prompted for a template for that environment. Related variables:

LaTeX-default-format   [User Option]
> Default format string for array and tabular environments.

LaTeX-default-width   [User Option]
> Default width for minipage and tabular* environments.

LaTeX-default-position   [User Option]
> Default position string for array and tabular environments. If nil, act like the empty
> string is given, but don't prompt for a position.

AUCTEX calculates the number of columns from the format string and inserts the suitable number of ampersands.

You can use *C-c LFD* (LaTeX-insert-item) to terminate rows in these environments. It
supplies line break macro '\\' and inserts the suitable number of ampersands on the next
line.

LaTeX-insert-item   [Command]
> (*C-c LFD*) Close the current row with '\\', move to the next line and insert an appro-
> priate number of ampersands for the current environment.

Similar supports are provided for various amsmath environments such as 'align',
'gather', 'alignat', 'matrix' etc. Try typing *C-c LFD* in these environments. It recog-
nizes the current environment and does the appropriate job depending on the context.

2.4.5 Customizing Environments

See Section 5.6.3 [Adding Environments], page 75, for how to customize the list of known
environments.

2.5 Entering Mathematics

TEX is written by a mathematician, and has always contained good support for formatting mathematical text. AUCTEX supports this tradition, by offering a special minor mode for entering text with many mathematical symbols. You can enter this mode by typing `C-c ~`.

LaTeX-math-mode [Command]

(`C-c ~`) Toggle LaTeX Math mode. This is a minor mode rebinding the key `LaTeX-math-abbrev-prefix` to allow easy typing of mathematical symbols. ' will read a character from the keyboard, and insert the symbol as specified in `LaTeX-math-default` and `LaTeX-math-list`. If given a prefix argument, the symbol will be surrounded by dollar signs.

You can use another prefix key (instead of ') by setting the variable `LaTeX-math-abbrev-prefix`.

To enable LaTeX Math mode by default, add the following in your `.emacs` file:

```
(add-hook 'LaTeX-mode-hook 'LaTeX-math-mode)
```

LaTeX-math-abbrev-prefix [User Option]

A string containing the prefix of `LaTeX-math-mode` commands; This value defaults to '.

The string has to be a key or key sequence in a format understood by the `kbd` macro. This corresponds to the syntax usually used in the manuals for Emacs Emacs Lisp.

The variable `LaTeX-math-list` allows you to add your own mappings.

LaTeX-math-list [User Option]

A list containing user-defined keys and commands to be used in LaTeX Math mode. Each entry should be a list of two to four elements.

First, the key to be used after `LaTeX-math-abbrev-prefix` for macro insertion. If it is nil, the symbol has no associated keystroke (it is available in the menu, though).

Second, a string representing the name of the macro (without a leading backslash.)

Third, a string representing the name of a submenu the command should be added to. Use a list of strings in case of nested menus.

Fourth, the position of a Unicode character to be displayed in the menu alongside the macro name. This is an integer value.

LaTeX-math-menu-unicode [User Option]

Whether the LaTeX menu should try using Unicode for effect. Your Emacs built must be able to display include Unicode characters in menus for this feature.

AUCTEX's reference card `tex-ref.tex` includes a list of all math mode commands.

AUCTEX can help you write subscripts and superscripts in math constructs by automatically inserting a pair of braces after typing _ or ^ respectively and putting point between the braces. In order to enable this feature, set the variable `TeX-electric-sub-and-superscript` to a non-nil value.

TeX-electric-sub-and-superscript [User Option]

If non-nil, insert braces after typing ^ and _ in math mode.

2.6 Completion

Emacs lisp programmers probably know the `lisp-complete-symbol` command, usually bound to *M-TAB*. Users of the wonderful ispell mode know and love the `ispell-complete-word` command from that package. Similarly, AUCTEX has a `TeX-complete-symbol` command, by default bound to *M-TAB* which is equivalent to *M-C-i*. Using `TeX-complete-symbol` makes it easier to type and remember the names of long LATEX macros.

In order to use `TeX-complete-symbol`, you should write a backslash and the start of the macro. Typing *M-TAB* will now complete as much of the macro, as it unambiguously can. For example, if you type "\renewc" and then *M-TAB*, it will expand to "\renewcommand".

`TeX-complete-symbol`   [Command]
>   (*M-TAB*) Complete TEX symbol before point.

A more direct way to insert a macro is with `TeX-insert-macro`, bound to *C-c C-m* which is equivalent to *C-c RET*. It has the advantage over completion that it knows about the argument of most standard LATEX macros, and will prompt for them. It also knows about the type of the arguments, so it will for example give completion for the argument to '\include'. Some examples are listed below.

`TeX-insert-macro`   [Command]
>   (*C-c C-m* or *C-c RET*) Prompt (with completion) for the name of a TEX macro, and if AUCTEX knows the macro, prompt for each argument.

As a default selection, AUCTEX will suggest the macro last inserted or, as the first choice the value of the variable `TeX-default-macro`.

`TeX-insert-macro-default-style`   [User Option]
>   Specifies whether `TeX-insert-macro` will ask for all optional arguments.
>
>   If set to the symbol `show-optional-args`, `TeX-insert-macro` asks for optional arguments of TEX marcos, unless the previous optional argument has been rejected. If set to `show-all-optional-args`, `TeX-insert-macro` asks for all optional arguments. `mandatory-args-only`, `TeX-insert-macro` asks only for mandatory arguments. When `TeX-insert-macro` is called with prefix argument (*C-u*), it's the other way round.
>
>   Note that for some macros, there are special mechanisms, e.g. `LaTeX-includegraphics-options-alist` and `TeX-arg-cite-note-p`.

`TeX-default-macro`   [User Option]
>   Default macro to insert when invoking `TeX-insert-macro` first time.

A faster alternative is to bind the function `TeX-electric-macro` to '\'. This can be done by setting the variable `TeX-electric-escape`

`TeX-electric-escape`   [User Option]
>   If this is non-nil when AUCTEX is loaded, the TEX escape character '\' will be bound to `TeX-electric-macro`

The difference between `TeX-insert-macro` and `TeX-electric-macro` is that space will complete and exit from the minibuffer in `TeX-electric-macro`. Use `TAB` if you merely want to complete.

TeX-electric-macro   [Command]

> Prompt (with completion) for the name of a TeX macro, and if AUCTeX knows the macro, prompt for each argument. Space will complete and exit.

By default AUCTeX will put an empty set braces '{}' after a macro with no arguments to stop it from eating the next whitespace. This can be stopped by entering `LaTeX-math-mode`, see Section 2.5 [Mathematics], page 30, or by setting `TeX-insert-braces` to nil.

TeX-insert-braces   [User Option]

> If non-nil, append a empty pair of braces after inserting a macro.

TeX-insert-braces-alist   [User Option]

> Control the insertion of a pair of braces after a macro on a per macro basis.
>
> This variable is an alist. Each element is a cons cell, whose car is the macro name, and the cdr is non-nil or nil, depending on whether a pair of braces should be, respectively, appended or not to the macro.
>
> If a macro has an element in this variable, `TeX-parse-macro` will use its value to decided what to do, whatever the value of the variable `TeX-insert-braces`.

Completions work because AUCTeX can analyze TeX files, and store symbols in Emacs Lisp files for later retrieval. See Section 5.5 [Automatic], page 67, for more information.

AUCTeX distinguishes normal and expert macros. By default, it will offer completion only for normal commands. This behavior can be controlled using the user option `TeX-complete-expert-commands`.

TeX-complete-expert-commands   [User Option]

> Complete macros and environments marked as expert commands.
>
> Possible values are nil, t, or a list of style names.
>
> nil   Don't complete expert commands (default).
>
> t   Always complete expert commands.
>
> (STYLES ...)
>   Only complete expert commands of STYLES.

AUCTeX will also make completion for many macro arguments, for example existing labels when you enter a '\ref' macro with `TeX-insert-macro` or `TeX-electric-macro`, and BibTeX entries when you enter a '\cite' macro. For this kind of completion to work, parsing must be enabled as described in see Section 5.3 [Parsing Files], page 62. For '\cite' you must also make sure that the BibTeX files have been saved at least once after you enabled automatic parsing on save, and that the basename of the BibTeX file does not conflict with the basename of one of TeX files.

2.7 Marking Environments, Sections, or Texinfo Nodes

You can mark the current environment by typing `C-c .`, or the current section by typing `C-c *`.

In Texinfo documents you can type `M-C-h` to mark the current node.

When the region is set, the point is moved to its beginning and the mark to its end.

2.7.1 LaTeX Commands for Marking Environments and Sections

`LaTeX-mark-section`   [Command]

(`C-c *`) Set mark at end of current logical section, and point at top.

With a non-nil prefix argument, mark only the region from the current section start to the next sectioning command. Thereby subsections are not being marked. Otherwise, any included subsections are also marked along with current section.

`LaTeX-mark-environment`   [Command]

(`C-c .`) Set mark to the end of the current environment and point to the matching beginning.

If a prefix argument is given, mark the respective number of enclosing environments. The command will not work properly if there are unbalanced begin-end pairs in comments and verbatim environments.

2.7.2 Texinfo Commands for Marking Environments and Sections

`Texinfo-mark-section`   [Command]

(`C-c *`) Mark the current section, with inclusion of any containing node.

The current section is detected as starting by any of the structuring commands matched by the regular expression in the variable `outline-regexp` which in turn is a regular expression matching any element of the variable `texinfo-section-list`.

With a non-nil prefix argument, mark only the region from the current section start to the next sectioning command. Thereby subsections are not being marked. Otherwise, any included subsections are also marked

Note that when the current section is starting immediately after a node command, then the node command is also marked as part of the section.

`Texinfo-mark-environment`   [Command]

(`C-c .`) Set mark to the end of the current environment and point to the matching beginning.

If a prefix argument is given, mark the respective number of enclosing environments. The command will not work properly if there are unbalanced begin-end pairs in comments and verbatim environments.

`Texinfo-mark-node`   [Command]

(`M-C-h`) Mark the current node. This is the node in which point is located. It is starting at the previous occurrence of the keyword `@node` and ending at next occurrence of the keywords `@node` or `@bye`.

2.8 Commenting

It is often necessary to comment out temporarily a region of TeX or LaTeX code. This can be done with the commands `C-c ;` and `C-c %`. `C-c ;` will comment out all lines in the current region, while `C-c %` will comment out the current paragraph. Type `C-c ;` again to uncomment all lines of a commented region, or `C-c %` again to uncomment all comment lines around point. These commands will insert or remove a single '`%`' respectively.

TeX-comment-or-uncomment-region   [Command]

(*C-c ;*) Add or remove '%' from the beginning of each line in the current region. Un-commenting works only if the region encloses solely commented lines. If AUCTEX should not try to guess if the region should be commented or uncommented the commands TeX-comment-region and TeX-uncomment-region can be used to explicitly comment or uncomment the region in concern.

TeX-comment-or-uncomment-paragraph   [Command]

(*C-c %*) Add or remove '%' from the beginning of each line in the current paragraph. When removing '%' characters the paragraph is considered to consist of all preceding and succeeding lines starting with a '%', until the first non-comment line.

2.9 Indenting

Indentation means the addition of whitespace at the beginning of lines to reflect special syntactical constructs. This makes it easier to see the structure of the document, and to catch errors such as a missing closing brace. Thus, the indentation is done for precisely the same reasons that you would indent ordinary computer programs.

Indentation is done by LaTeX environments and by TeX groups, that is the body of an environment is indented by the value of LaTeX-indent-level (default 2). Also, items of an 'itemize-like' environment are indented by the value of LaTeX-item-indent, default −2. (Items are identified with the help of LaTeX-item-regexp.) If more environments are nested, they are indented 'accumulated' just like most programming languages usually are seen indented in nested constructs.

You can explicitly indent single lines, usually by pressing TAB, or marked regions by calling indent-region on it. If you have auto-fill-mode enabled and a line is broken while you type it, Emacs automatically cares about the indentation in the following line. If you want to have a similar behavior upon typing RET, you can customize the variable TeX-newline-function and change the default of newline which does no indentation to newline-and-indent which indents the new line or reindent-then-newline-and-indent which indents both the current and the new line.

There are certain LaTeX environments which should be indented in a special way, like 'tabular' or 'verbatim'. Those environments may be specified in the variable LaTeX-indent-environment-list together with their special indentation functions. Taking the 'verbatim' environment as an example you can see that current-indentation is used as the indentation function. This will stop AUCTEX from doing any indentation in the environment if you hit TAB for example.

There are environments in LaTeX-indent-environment-list which do not bring a special indentation function with them. This is due to the fact that first the respective functions are not implemented yet and second that filling will be disabled for the specified environments. This shall prevent the source code from being messed up by accidently filling those environments with the standard filling routine. If you think that providing special filling routines for such environments would be an appropriate and challenging task for you, you are invited to contribute. (See Section 2.10 [Filling], page 36, for further information about the filling functionality)

The check for the indentation function may be enabled or disabled by customizing the variable LaTeX-indent-environment-check.

As a side note with regard to formatting special environments: Newer Emacsen include `align.el` and therefore provide some support for formatting 'tabular' and 'tabbing' environments with the function `align-current` which will nicely align columns in the source code.

AUCTeX is able to format commented parts of your code just as any other part. This means LaTeX environments and TeX groups in comments will be indented syntactically correct if the variable `LaTeX-syntactic-comments` is set to t. If you disable it, comments will be filled like normal text and no syntactic indentation will be done.

Following you will find a list of most commands and variables related to indenting with a small summary in each case:

TAB   `LaTeX-indent-line` will indent the current line.

LFD   `newline-and-indent` inserts a new line (much like `RET`) and moves the cursor to an appropriate position by the left margin.

         Most keyboards nowadays lack a linefeed key and `C-j` may be tedious to type. Therefore you can customize AUCTeX to perform indentation upon typing `RET` as well. The respective option is called `TeX-newline-function`.

`C-j`   Alias for LFD

LaTeX-indent-environment-list [User Option]

List of environments with special indentation. The second element in each entry is the function to calculate the indentation level in columns.

The filling code currently cannot handle tabular-like environments which will be completely messed-up if you try to format them. This is why most of these environments are included in this customization option without a special indentation function. This will prevent that they get filled.

LaTeX-indent-level [User Option]

Number of spaces to add to the indentation for each '`\begin`' not matched by a '`\end`'.

LaTeX-item-indent [User Option]

Number of spaces to add to the indentation for '`\item`''s in list environments.

TeX-brace-indent-level [User Option]

Number of spaces to add to the indentation for each '{' not matched by a '}'.

LaTeX-syntactic-comments [User Option]

If non-nil comments will be filled and indented according to LaTeX syntax. Otherwise they will be filled like normal text.

TeX-newline-function [User Option]

Used to specify the function which is called when `RET` is pressed. This will normally be `newline` which simply inserts a new line. In case you want to have AUCTeX do indentation as well when you press `RET`, use the built-in functions `newline-and-indent` or `reindent-then-newline-and-indent`. The former inserts a new line and indents the following line, i.e. it moves the cursor to the right position and therefore acts as if you pressed LFD. The latter function additionally indents the current line. If you choose '`Other`', you can specify your own fancy function to be called when `RET` is pressed.

2.10 Filling

Filling deals with the insertion of line breaks to prevent lines from becoming wider than what is specified in `fill-column`. The linebreaks will be inserted automatically if `auto-fill-mode` is enabled. In this case the source is not only filled but also indented automatically as you write it.

`auto-fill-mode` can be enabled for AUCTEX by calling `turn-on-auto-fill` in one of the hooks AUCTEX is running. See Section 5.1 [Modes and Hooks], page 60. As an example, if you want to enable `auto-fill-mode` in `LaTeX-mode`, put the following into your init file:

```
(add-hook 'LaTeX-mode-hook 'turn-on-auto-fill)
```

You can manually fill explicitly marked regions, paragraphs, environments, complete sections, or the whole buffer. (Note that manual filling in AUCTEX will indent the start of the region to be filled in contrast to many other Emacs modes.)

There are some syntactical constructs which are handled specially with regard to filling. These are so-called code comments and paragraph commands.

Code comments are comments preceded by code or text in the same line. Upon filling a region, code comments themselves will not get filled. Filling is done from the start of the region to the line with the code comment and continues after it. In order to prevent overfull lines in the source code, a linebreak will be inserted before the last non-comment word by default. This can be changed by customizing `LaTeX-fill-break-before-code-comments`. If you have overfull lines with code comments you can fill those explicitly by calling `LaTeX-fill-paragraph` or pressing `M-q` with the cursor positioned on them. This will add linebreaks in the comment and indent subsequent comment lines to the column of the comment in the first line of the code comment. In this special case `M-q` only acts on the current line and not on the whole paragraph.

Lines with '`\par`' are treated similarly to code comments, i.e. '`\par`' will be treated as paragraph boundary which should not be followed by other code or text. But it is not treated as a real paragraph boundary like an empty line where filling a paragraph would stop.

Paragraph commands like '`\section`' or '`\noindent`' (the list of commands is defined by `LaTeX-paragraph-commands`) are often to be placed in their own line(s). This means they should not be consecuted with any preceding or following adjacent lines of text. AUCTEX will prevent this from happening if you do not put any text except another macro after the end of the last brace of the respective macro. If there is other text after the macro, AUCTEX regards this as a sign that the macro is part of the following paragraph.

Here are some examples:

```
\begin{quote}
  text text text text
\begin{quote}\label{foo}
  text text text text
```

If you press `M-q` on the first line in both examples, nothing will change. But if you write

```
\begin{quote} text
  text text text text
```

and press `M-q`, you will get

```
\begin{quote} text text text text text
```
Besides code comments and paragraph commands, another speciality of filling in AUCTEX involves commented lines. You should be aware that these comments are treated as islands in the rest of the LaTeX code if syntactic filling is enabled. This means, for example, if you try to fill an environment with `LaTeX-fill-environment` and have the cursor placed on a commented line which does not have a surrounding environment inside the comment, AUCTEX will report an error.

The relevant commands and variables with regard to filling are:

C-c C-q C-p

> `LaTeX-fill-paragraph` will fill and indent the current paragraph.

M-q   Alias for *C-c C-q C-p*

C-c C-q C-e

> `LaTeX-fill-environment` will fill and indent the current environment. This may e.g. be the 'document' environment, in which case the entire document will be formatted.

C-c C-q C-s

> `LaTeX-fill-section` will fill and indent the current logical sectional unit.

C-c C-q C-r

> `LaTeX-fill-region` will fill and indent the current region.

LaTeX-fill-break-at-separators   [User Option]

> List of separators before or after which respectively linebreaks will be inserted if they do not fit into one line. The separators can be curly braces, brackets, switches for inline math ('$', '\(', '\)') and switches for display math ('\[', '\]'). Such formatting can be useful to make macros and math more visible or to prevent overfull lines in the LaTeX source in case a package for displaying formatted TeX output inside the Emacs buffer, like preview-latex, is used.

LaTeX-fill-break-before-code-comments   [User Option]

> Code comments are comments preceded by some other text in the same line. When a paragraph containing such a comment is to be filled, the comment start will be seen as a border after which no line breaks will be inserted in the same line. If the option **LaTeX-fill-break-before-code-comments** is enabled (which is the default) and the comment does not fit into the line, a line break will be inserted before the last non-comment word to minimize the chance that the line becomes overfull.

3 Controlling Screen Display

It is often desirable to get visual help of what markup code in a text actually does without having to decipher it explicitly. For this purpose Emacs and AUCTeX provide font locking (also known as syntax highlighting) which visually sets off markup code like macros or environments by using different colors or fonts. For example text to be typeset in italics can be displayed with an italic font in the editor as well, or labels and references get their own distinct color.

While font locking helps you grasp the purpose of markup code and separate markup from content, the markup code can still be distracting. AUCTeX lets you hide those parts and show them again at request with its built-in support for hiding macros and environments which we call folding here.

Besides folding of macros and environments, AUCTeX provides support for Emacs' outline mode which lets you narrow the buffer content to certain sections of your text by hiding the parts not belonging to these sections.

Moreover, you can focus in a specific portion of the code by narrowing the buffer to the desired region. AUCTeX provides also functions to narrow the buffer to the current group and to LaTeX environments.

3.1 Font Locking

Font locking is supposed to improve readability of the source code by highlighting certain keywords with different colors or fonts. It thereby lets you recognize the function of markup code to a certain extent without having to read the markup command. For general information on controlling font locking with Emacs' Font Lock mode, see Section "Font Lock Mode" in *GNU Emacs Manual*.

TeX-install-font-lock   [User Option]
> Once font locking is enabled globally or for the major modes provided by AUCTeX, the font locking patterns and functionality of **font-latex** are activated by default. You can switch to a different font locking scheme or disable font locking in AUCTeX by customizing the variable `TeX-install-font-lock`.
>
> Besides **font-latex** AUCTeX ships with a scheme which is derived from Emacs' default LaTeX mode and activated by choosing `tex-font-setup`. Be aware that this scheme is not coupled with AUCTeX's style system and not the focus of development. Therefore and due to **font-latex** being much more feature-rich the following explanations will only cover **font-latex**.
>
> In case you want to hook in your own fontification scheme, you can choose **other** and insert the name of the function which sets up your font locking patterns. If you want to disable fontification in AUCTeX completely, choose **ignore**.

font-latex provides many options for customization which are accessible with `M-x customize-group RET font-latex RET`. For this description the various options are explained in conceptional groups.

3.1.1 Fontification of macros

Highlighting of macros can be customized by adapting keyword lists which can be found in the customization group `font-latex-keywords`.

Three types of macros can be handled differently with respect to fontification:

1. Commands of the form '`\foo[bar]{baz}`' which consist of the macro itself, optional arguments in square brackets and mandatory arguments in curly braces. For the command itself the face `font-lock-keyword-face` will be used and for the optional arguments the face `font-lock-variable-name-face`. The face applied to the mandatory argument depends on the macro class represented by the respective built-in variables.

2. Declaration macros of the form '`{\foo text}`' which consist of the macro which may be enclosed in a TeX group together with text to be affected by the macro. In case a TeX group is present, the macro will get the face `font-lock-keyword-face` and the text will get the face configured for the respective macro class. If no TeX group is present, the latter face will be applied to the macro itself.

3. Simple macros of the form '`\foo`' which do not have any arguments or groupings. The respective face will be applied to the macro itself.

Customization variables for '`\foo[bar]{baz}`' type macros allow both the macro name and the sequence of arguments to be specified. The latter is done with a string which can contain the characters

'`*`'	indicating the existence of a starred variant for the macro,
'`[`'	for optional arguments in brackets,
'`{`'	for mandatory arguments in braces,
'`\`'	for mandatory arguments consisting of a single macro and
'`|`'	as a prefix indicating that two alternatives are following.

For example the specifier for '`\documentclass`' would be '`[{`' because the macro has one optional followed by one mandatory argument. The specifier for '`\newcommand`' would be '`*|{\[[{`' because there is a starred variant, the mandatory argument following the macro name can be a macro or a TeX group which can be followed by two optional arguments and the last token is a mandatory argument in braces.

Customization variables for the '`{\foo text}`' and '`\foo`' types are simple lists of strings where each entry is a macro name (without the leading backslash).

General macro classes

font-latex provides keyword lists for different macro classes which are described in the following table:

`font-latex-match-function-keywords`
> Keywords for macros defining or related to functions, like '`\newcommand`'.
> Type: '`\macro[...]{...}`'
> Face: `font-lock-function-name-face`

`font-latex-match-reference-keywords`
> Keywords for macros defining or related to references, like '`\ref`'.
> Type: '`\macro[...]{...}`'
> Face: `font-lock-constant-face`

`font-latex-match-textual-keywords`

> Keywords for macros specifying textual content, like '`\caption`'.
> Type: '`\macro[...]{...}`'
> Face: `font-lock-type-face`

`font-latex-match-variable-keywords`

> Keywords for macros defining or related to variables, like '`\setlength`'.
> Type: '`\macro[...]{...}`'
> Face: `font-lock-variable-name-face`

`font-latex-match-warning-keywords`

> Keywords for important macros, e.g. affecting line or page break, like
> '`\clearpage`'.
> Type: '`\macro`'
> Face: `font-latex-warning-face`

Sectioning commands

Sectioning commands are macros like '`\chapter`' or '`\section`'. For these commands
there are two fontification schemes which may be selected by customizing the variable
`font-latex-fontify-sectioning`.

`font-latex-fontify-sectioning`   [User Option]

> Per default sectioning commands will be shown in a larger, proportional font, which
> corresponds to a number for this variable. The font size varies with the section-
> ing level, e.g. '`\part`' (`font-latex-sectioning-0-face`) has a larger font than
> '`\paragraph`' (`font-latex-sectioning-5-face`). Typically, values from 1.05 to 1.3
> for `font-latex-fontify-sectioning` give best results, depending on your font setup.
> If you rather like to use the base font and a different color, set the variable to the
> symbol '`color`'. In this case the face `font-lock-type-face` will be used to fontify
> the argument of the sectioning commands.

You can make font-latex aware of your own sectioning commands be adding them to the
keyword lists: `font-latex-match-sectioning-0-keywords` (`font-latex-sectioning-0-face`) ... `font-latex-match-sectioning-5-keywords` (`font-latex-sectioning-5-face`).

Related to sectioning there is special support for slide titles which may be fontified with
the face `font-latex-slide-title-face`. You can add macros which should appear in this
face by customizing the variable `font-latex-match-slide-title-keywords`.

Commands for changing fonts

LaTeX provides various macros for changing fonts or font attributes. For example, you can
select an italic font with '`\textit{...}`' or bold with '`\textbf{...}`'. An alternative way
to specify these fonts is to use special macros in TeX groups, like '`{\itshape ...}`' for
italics and '`{\bfseries ...}`' for bold. As mentioned above, we call the former variants
commands and the latter declarations.

Besides the macros for changing fonts provided by LaTeX there is an infinite number of
other macros—either defined by yourself for logical markup or defined by macro packages—
which affect the font in the typeset text. While LaTeX's built-in macros and macros of

packages known by AUCTeX are already handled by font-latex, different keyword lists per type style and macro type are provided for entering your own macros which are listed in the table below.

`font-latex-match-bold-command-keywords`
>   Keywords for commands specifying a bold type style.
>   Face: `font-latex-bold-face`

`font-latex-match-italic-command-keywords`
>   Keywords for commands specifying an italic font.
>   Face: `font-latex-italic-face`

`font-latex-match-math-command-keywords`
>   Keywords for commands specifying a math font.
>   Face: `font-latex-math-face`

`font-latex-match-type-command-keywords`
>   Keywords for commands specifying a typewriter font.
>   Face: `font-lock-type-face`

`font-latex-match-bold-declaration-keywords`
>   Keywords for declarations specifying a bold type style.
>   Face: `font-latex-bold-face`

`font-latex-match-italic-declaration-keywords`
>   Keywords for declarations specifying an italic font.
>   Face: `font-latex-italic-face`

`font-latex-match-type-declaration-keywords`
>   Keywords for declarations specifying a typewriter font.
>   Face: `font-latex-type-face`

Deactivating defaults of built-in keyword classes

font-latex ships with predefined lists of keywords for the classes described above. You can disable these defaults per class by customizing the variable `font-latex-deactivated-keyword-classes`. This is a list of strings for keyword classes to be deactivated. Valid entries are "warning", "variable", "reference", "function" , "sectioning-0", "sectioning-1", "sectioning-2", "sectioning-3", "sectioning-4", "sectioning-5", "textual", "bold-command", "italic-command", "math-command", "type-command", "bold-declaration", "italic-declaration", "type-declaration".

You can also get rid of certain keywords only. For example if you want to remove highlighting of footnotes as references you can put the following stanza into your init file:

```
(eval-after-load "font-latex"
  '(setq-default
    font-latex-match-reference-keywords-local
    (remove "footnote" font-latex-match-reference-keywords-local)))
```

But note that this means fiddling with font-latex's internals and is not guaranteed to work in future versions of font-latex.

User-defined keyword classes

In case the customization options explained above do not suffice for your needs, you can specify your own keyword classes by customizing the variable `font-latex-user-keyword-classes`.

`font-latex-user-keyword-classes`   [User Option]
>   Every keyword class consists of four parts, a name, a list of keywords, a face and a specifier for the type of macros to be highlighted.
>
>   When adding new entries, you have to use unique values for the class names, i.e. they must not clash with names of the built-in keyword classes or other names given by you. Additionally the names must not contain spaces.
>
>   The list of keywords defines which commands and declarations should be covered by the keyword class. A keyword can either be a simple command name omitting the leading backslash or a list consisting of the command name and a string specifying the sequence of arguments for the command.
>
>   The face argument can either be an existing face or font specifications made by you. (The latter option is not available on XEmacs.)
>
>   There are three alternatives for the type of keywords—"Command with arguments", "Declaration inside TEX group" and "Command without arguments"—which correspond with the macro types explained above.

3.1.2 Fontification of quotes

Text in quotation marks is displayed with the face `font-latex-string-face`. Besides the various forms of opening and closing double and single quotation marks, so-called guillemets (<<, >>) can be used for quoting. Because there are two styles of using them—French style: << text >>; German style: >>text<<—you can customize the variable `font-latex-quotes` to tell font-latex which type you are using if the correct value cannot be derived from document properties.

`font-latex-quotes`   [User Option]
>   The default value of `font-latex-quotes` is 'auto' which means that font-latex will try to derive the correct type of quotation mark matching from document properties like the language option supplied to the babel LATEX package.
>
>   If the automatic detection fails for you and you mostly use one specific style you can set it to a specific language-dependent value as well. Set the value to 'german' if you are using >>German quotes<< and to 'french' if you are using << French quotes >>. font-latex will recognize the different ways these quotes can be given in your source code, i.e. ('"<', '">'), ('<<', '>>') and the respective 8-bit variants.
>
>   If you set `font-latex-quotes` to nil, quoted content will not be fontified.

3.1.3 Fontification of mathematical constructs

In LATEX mathematics can be indicated by a variety of different methods: toggles (like dollar signs), macros and environments. Math constructs known by font-latex are displayed with the face `font-latex-math-face`. Support for dollar signs and shorthands like '\(...\)'

or '\[...\]' is built-in and not customizable. Support for other math macros and environments can be adapted by customizing the variables `font-latex-match-math-command-keywords` and `font-latex-math-environments` respectively.

In order to make math constructs more readable, font-latex displays subscript and superscript parts in a smaller font and raised or lowered respectively. This fontification feature can be controlled with the variables `font-latex-fontify-script` and `font-latex-script-display`.

`font-latex-fontify-script`   [User Option]
> If non-nil, fontify subscript and superscript strings.
>
> Note that this feature is not available on XEmacs, for which it is disabled per default. In GNU Emacs raising and lowering is not enabled for versions 21.3 and before due to it working not properly.

`font-latex-script-display`   [User Option]
> Display specification for subscript and superscript content. The car is used for subscript, the cdr is used for superscript. The feature is implemented using so-called display properties. For information on what exactly to specify for the values, see Section "Other Display Specifications" in *GNU Emacs Lisp Reference Manual*.

3.1.4 Verbatim macros and environments

Usually it is not desirable to have content to be typeset verbatim highlighted according to LaTeX syntax. Therefore this content will be fontified uniformly with the face `font-latex-verbatim-face`.

font-latex differentiates three different types of verbatim constructs for fontification. Macros with special characters like | as delimiters, macros with braces, and environments. Which macros and environments are recognized is controlled by the variables `LaTeX-verbatim-macros-with-delims`, `LaTeX-verbatim-macros-with-braces`, and `LaTeX-verbatim-environments` respectively.

3.1.5 Faces used by font-latex

In case you want to change the colors and fonts used by font-latex please refer to the faces mentioned in the explanations above and use *M-x customize-face RET <face> RET*. All faces defined by font-latex are accessible through a customization group by typing *M-x customize-group RET font-latex-highlighting-faces RET*.

3.1.6 Known fontification problems

In certain cases the fontification machinery fails to interpret buffer contents correctly. This can lead to color bleed, i.e. large parts of a buffer get fontified with an inappropriate face. A typical situation for this to happen is the use of a dollar sign ('$') in a verbatim macro or environment. If font-latex is not aware of the verbatim construct, it assumes the dollar sign to be a toggle for mathematics and fontifies the following buffer content with the respective face until it finds a closing dollar sign or till the end of the buffer.

As a remedy you can make the verbatim construct known to font-latex, see Section 3.1.4 [Verbatim content], page 43. If this is not possible, you can insert a commented dollar sign ('%$') at the next suitable end of line as a quick workaround.

3.2 Folding Macros and Environments

A popular complaint about markup languages like TeX and LaTeX is that there is too much clutter in the source text and that one cannot focus well on the content. There are macros where you are only interested in the content they are enclosing, like font specifiers where the content might already be fontified in a special way by font locking. Or macros the content of which you only want to see when actually editing it, like footnotes or citations. Similarly you might find certain environments or comments distracting when trying to concentrate on the body of your document.

With AUCTeX's folding functionality you can collapse those items and replace them by a fixed string, the content of one of their arguments, or a mixture of both. If you want to make the original text visible again in order to view or edit it, move point sideways onto the placeholder (also called display string) or left-click with the mouse pointer on it. (The latter is currently only supported on Emacs.) The macro or environment will unfold automatically, stay open as long as point is inside of it and collapse again once you move point out of it. (Note that folding of environments currently does not work in every AUCTeX mode.)

In order to use this feature, you have to activate `TeX-fold-mode` which will activate the auto-reveal feature and the necessary commands to hide and show macros and environments. You can activate the mode in a certain buffer by typing the command *M-x TeX-fold-mode RET* or using the keyboard shortcut *C-c C-o C-f*. If you want to use it every time you edit a LaTeX document, add it to a hook:

```
(add-hook 'LaTeX-mode-hook (lambda ()
                             (TeX-fold-mode 1)))
```

If it should be activated in all AUCTeX modes, use `TeX-mode-hook` instead of `LaTeX-mode-hook`.

Once the mode is active there are several commands available to hide and show macros, environments and comments:

TeX-fold-buffer   [Command]

> (*C-c C-o C-b*) Hide all foldable items in the current buffer according to the setting of `TeX-fold-type-list`.
>
> If you want to have this done automatically every time you open a file, add it to a hook and make sure the function is called after font locking is set up for the buffer. The following code should accomplish this:
>
> ```
> (add-hook 'find-file-hook 'TeX-fold-buffer t)
> ```
>
> The command can be used any time to refresh the whole buffer and fold any new macros and environments which were inserted after the last invocation of the command.

TeX-fold-type-list   [User Option]

> List of symbols determining the item classes to consider for folding. This can be macros, environments and comments. Per default only macros and environments are folded.

TeX-fold-force-fontify   [User Option]
> In order for all folded content to get the right faces, the whole buffer has to be fontified before folding is carried out. `TeX-fold-buffer` therefore will force fontification of unfontified regions. As this will prolong the time folding takes, you can prevent forced fontification by customizing the variable `TeX-fold-force-fontify`.

TeX-fold-auto   [User Option]
> By default, a macro inserted with `TeX-insert-macro` (*C-c C-m*) will not be folded. Set this variable to a non-nil value to aumatically fold macros as soon as they are inserted.

TeX-fold-preserve-comments   [User Option]
> By default items found in comments will be folded. If your comments often contain unfinished code this might lead to problems. Give this variable a non-nil value and foldable items in your comments will be left alone.

TeX-fold-unfold-around-mark   [User Option]
> When this variable is non-nil and there is an active regione, text around the mark will be kept unfolded.

TeX-fold-region   [Command]
> (*C-c C-o C-r*) Hide all configured macros in the marked region.

TeX-fold-paragraph   [Command]
> (*C-c C-o C-p*) Hide all configured macros in the paragraph containing point.

TeX-fold-macro   [Command]
> (*C-c C-o C-m*) Hide the macro on which point currently is located. If the name of the macro is found in `TeX-fold-macro-spec-list`, the respective display string will be shown instead. If it is not found, the name of the macro in sqare brackets or the default string for unspecified macros (`TeX-fold-unspec-macro-display-string`) will be shown, depending on the value of the variable `TeX-fold-unspec-use-name`.

TeX-fold-env   [Command]
> (*C-c C-o C-e*) Hide the environment on which point currently is located. The behavior regarding the display string is analogous to `TeX-fold-macro` and determined by the variables `TeX-fold-env-spec-list` and `TeX-fold-unspec-env-display-string` respectively.

TeX-fold-math   [Command]
> Hide the math macro on which point currently is located. If the name of the macro is found in `TeX-fold-math-spec-list`, the respective display string will be shown instead. If it is not found, the name of the macro in sqare brackets or the default string for unspecified macros (`TeX-fold-unspec-macro-display-string`) will be shown, depending on the value of the variable `TeX-fold-unspec-use-name`.

TeX-fold-comment   [Command]
> (*C-c C-o C-c*) Hide the comment point is located on.

TeX-fold-clearout-buffer   [Command]
> (*C-c C-o b*) Permanently unfold all macros and environments in the current buffer.

TeX-fold-clearout-region   [Command]

    (*C-c C-o r*) Permanently unfold all macros and environments in the marked region.

TeX-fold-clearout-paragraph   [Command]

    (*C-c C-o p*) Permanently unfold all macros and environments in the paragraph containing point.

TeX-fold-clearout-item   [Command]

    (*C-c C-o i*) Permanently show the macro or environment on which point currently is located. In contrast to temporarily opening the macro when point is moved sideways onto it, the macro will be permanently unfolded and will not collapse again once point is leaving it.

TeX-fold-dwim   [Command]

    (*C-c C-o C-o*) Hide or show items according to the current context. If there is folded content, unfold it. If there is a marked region, fold all configured content in this region. If there is no folded content but a macro or environment, fold it.

In case you want to use a different prefix than *C-c C-o* for these commands you can customize the variable **TeX-fold-command-prefix**. (Note that this will not change the key binding for activating the mode.)

The commands above will only take macros or environments into consideration which are specified in the variables **TeX-fold-macro-spec-list** or **TeX-fold-env-spec-list** respectively.

TeX-fold-macro-spec-list   [User Option]

    List of replacement specifiers and macros to fold. The specifier can be a string, an integer or a function symbol.

    If you specify a string, it will be used as a display replacement for the whole macro. Numbers in braces, brackets, parens or angle brackets will be replaced by the respective macro argument. For example '{1}' will be replaced by the first mandatory argument of the macro. One can also define alternatives within the specifier which are used if an argument is not found. Alternatives are separated by '||'. They are most useful with optional arguments. As an example, the default specifier for '\item' is '[1]:||*' which means that if there is an optional argument, its value is shown followed by a colon. If there is no optional argument, only an asterisk is used as the display string.

    If you specify a number as the first element, the content of the respective mandatory argument of a LaTeX macro will be used as the placeholder.

    If the first element is a function symbol, the function will be called with all mandatory arguments of the macro and the result of the function call will be used as a replacement for the macro.

    The placeholder is made by copying the text from the buffer together with its properties, i.e. its face as well. If fontification has not happened when this is done (e.g. because of lazy font locking) the intended fontification will not show up. As a workaround you can leave Emacs idle a few seconds and wait for stealth font locking to finish before you fold the buffer. Or you just re-fold the buffer with **TeX-fold-buffer** when you notice a wrong fontification.

`TeX-fold-env-spec-list`   [User Option]
>   List of display strings or argument numbers and environments to fold. Argument numbers refer to the '`\begin`' statement. That means if you have e.g. '`\begin{tabularx}{\linewidth}{XXX} ... \end{tabularx}`' and specify 3 as the argument number, the resulting display string will be "XXX".

`TeX-fold-math-spec-list`   [User Option]
>   List of display strings and math macros to fold.

The variables `TeX-fold-macro-spec-list`, `TeX-fold-env-spec-list`, and `TeX-fold-math-spec-list` apply to any AUCTeX mode. If you want to make settings which are only applied to LaTeX mode, you can use the mode-specific variables `LaTeX-fold-macro-spec-list`, `LaTeX-fold-env-spec-list`, and `LaTeX-fold-math-spec-list`

`TeX-fold-unspec-macro-display-string`   [User Option]
>   Default display string for macros which are not specified in `TeX-fold-macro-spec-list`.

`TeX-fold-unspec-env-display-string`   [User Option]
>   Default display string for environments which are not specified in `TeX-fold-env-spec-list`.

`TeX-fold-unspec-use-name`   [User Option]
>   If non-nil the name of the macro or environment surrounded by square brackets is used as display string, otherwise the defaults specified in `TeX-fold-unspec-macro-display-string` or `TeX-fold-unspec-env-display-string` respectively.

When you hover with the mouse pointer over folded content, its original text will be shown in a tooltip or the echo area depending on Tooltip mode being activate. In order to avoid exorbitantly big tooltips and to cater for the limited space in the echo area the content will be cropped after a certain amount of characters defined by the variable `TeX-fold-help-echo-max-length`.

`TeX-fold-help-echo-max-length`   [User Option]
>   Maximum length of original text displayed in a tooltip or the echo area for folded content. Set it to zero in order to disable this feature.

3.3 Outlining the Document

AUCTeX supports the standard outline minor mode using LaTeX/ConTeXt sectioning commands as header lines. See Section "Outline Mode" in *GNU Emacs Manual*.

You can add your own headings by setting the variable `TeX-outline-extra`.

`TeX-outline-extra`   [Variable]
>   List of extra TeX outline levels.
>
>   Each element is a list with two entries. The first entry is the regular expression matching a header, and the second is the level of the header. A '`^`' is automatically prepended to the regular expressions in the list, so they must match text at the beginning of the line.
>
>   See `LaTeX-section-list` or `ConTeXt-INTERFACE-section-list` for existing header levels.

The following example add '\item' and '\bibliography' headers, with '\bibliography' at the same outline level as '\section', and '\item' being below '\subparagraph'.

```
(setq TeX-outline-extra
      '(("[ \t]*\\\\\\(bib\\)?item\\b" 7)
("\\\\bibliography\\b" 2)))
```

You may want to check out the unbundled **out-xtra** package for even better outline support. It is available from your favorite emacs lisp archive.

3.4 Narrowing

Sometimes you want to focus your attention to a limited region of the code. You can do that by restricting the text addressable by editing commands and hiding the rest of the buffer with the narrowing functions, see Section "Narrowing" in *GNU Emacs Manual*. In addition, AUCTeX provides a couple of other commands to narrow the buffer to a group, i.e. a region enclosed in a pair of curly braces, and to LaTeX environments.

TeX-narrow-to-group   [Command]
    (*C-x n g*) Make text outside current group invisible.

LaTeX-narrow-to-environment *count*   [Command]
    (*C-x n e*) Make text outside current environment invisible. With optional argument *count* keep visible that number of enclosing environmens.

Like other standard narrowing functions, the above commands are disabled. Attempting to use them asks for confirmation and gives you the option of enabling them; if you enable the commands, confirmation will no longer be required for them.

4 Starting Processors, Viewers and Other Programs

The most powerful features of AUCTEX may be those allowing you to run TEX, LATEX, ConTEXt and other external commands like BibTEX and `makeindex` from within Emacs, viewing and printing the results, and moreover allowing you to *debug* your documents.

AUCTEX comes with a special tool bar for TEX and LATEX which provides buttons for the most important commands. You can enable or disable it by customizing the options `plain-TeX-enable-toolbar` and `LaTeX-enable-toolbar` in the `TeX-tool-bar` customization group.

4.1 Executing Commands

Formatting the document with TEX, LATEX or ConTEXt, viewing with a previewer, printing the document, running BibTEX, making an index, or checking the document with `lacheck` or `chktex` all require running an external command.

4.1.1 Starting a Command on a Document or Region

There are two ways to run an external command, you can either run it on the current document with `TeX-command-master`, or on the current region with `TeX-command-region`. A special case of running TEX on a region is `TeX-command-buffer` which differs from `TeX-command-master` if the current buffer is not its own master file.

`TeX-command-master`   [Command]

     (*C-c C-c*) Query the user for a command, and run it on the master file associated with the current buffer. The name of the master file is controlled by the variable `TeX-master`. The available commands are controlled by the variable `TeX-command-list`.

`TeX-command-region`   [Command]

     (*C-c C-r*) Query the user for a command, and run it on the contents of the selected region. The region contents are written into the region file, after extracting the header and trailer from the master file. If mark is inactive (which can happen with Transient Mark mode), use the old region. See also the command `TeX-pin-region` about how to fix a region.

     The name of the region file is controlled by the variable `TeX-region`. The name of the master file is controlled by the variable `TeX-master`. The header is all text up to the line matching the regular expression `TeX-header-end`. The trailer is all text from the line matching the regular expression `TeX-trailer-start`. The available commands are controlled by the variable `TeX-command-list`.

`TeX-command-buffer`   [Command]

     (*C-c C-b*) Query the user for a command, and apply it to the contents of the current buffer. The buffer contents are written into the region file, after extracting the header and trailer from the master file. The command is then actually run on the region file. See above for details.

`TeX-region`   [User Option]

     The name of the file for temporarily storing the text when formatting the current region.

TeX-header-end [User Option]

A regular expression matching the end of the header. By default, this is '\begin{document}' in LaTeX mode and '%**end of header' in TeX mode.

TeX-trailer-start [User Option]

A regular expression matching the start of the trailer. By default, this is '\end{document}' in LaTeX mode and '\bye' in TeX mode.

If you want to change the values of **TeX-header-end** and **TeX-trailer-start** you can do this for all files by setting the variables in a mode hook or per file by specifying them as file variables (see Section "File Variables" in *The Emacs Editor*).

TeX-pin-region [Command]

(*C-c C-t C-r*) If you don't have a mode like Transient Mark mode active, where marks get disabled automatically, the region would need to get properly set before each call to **TeX-command-region**. If you fix the current region with *C-c C-t C-r*, then it will get used for more commands even though mark and point may change. An explicitly activated mark, however, will always define a new region when calling **TeX-command-region**.

AUCTeX will allow one process for each document, plus one process for the region file to be active at the same time. Thus, if you are editing *n* different documents, you can have *n* plus one processes running at the same time. If the last process you started was on the region, the commands described in Section 4.3 [Debugging], page 56 and Section 4.5 [Control], page 58 will work on that process, otherwise they will work on the process associated with the current document.

4.1.2 Selecting and Executing a Command

Once you started the command selection with *C-c C-c*, *C-c C-s* or *C-c C-b* you will be prompted for the type of command. AUCTeX will try to guess which command is appropriate in the given situation and propose it as default. Usually this is a processor like 'TeX' or 'LaTeX' if the document was changed or a viewer if the document was just typeset. Other commands can be selected in the minibuffer with completion support by typing **TAB**.

The available commands are defined by the variable **TeX-command-list**. Per default it includes commands for typesetting the document (e.g. 'LaTeX'), for viewing the output ('View'), for printing ('Print'), for generating an index ('Index') or for spell checking ('Spell') to name but a few. You can also add your own commands by adding entries to **TeX-command-list**. Refer to its doc string for information about its syntax. You might also want to look at **TeX-expand-list** to learn about the expanders you can use in **TeX-command-list**.

Note that the default of the variable occasionally changes. Therefore it is advisable to add to the list rather than overwriting it. You can do this with a call to **add-to-list** in your init file. For example, if you wanted to add a command for running a program called 'foo' on the master or region file, you could do this with the following form.

```
(eval-after-load "tex"
  '(add-to-list 'TeX-command-list
'("Foo" "foo %s" TeX-run-command t t :help "Run foo") t))
```

As mentioned before, AUCTeX will try to guess what command you want to invoke. If you want to use another command than 'TeX', 'LaTeX' or whatever processor AUCTeX thinks is appropriate for the current mode, set the variable `TeX-command-default`. You can do this for all files by setting it in a mode hook or per file by specifying it as a file variable (see Section "File Variables" in *The Emacs Editor*).

`TeX-command-default`   [User Option]
> The default command to run in this buffer. Must be an entry in `TeX-command-list`.

In case you use biblatex in a document, when automatic parsing is enabled AUCTeX checks the value of 'backend' option given to biblatex at load time to decide whether to use BibTeX or Biber for bibliography processing. Should AUCTeX fail to detect the right backend, you can use the file local `LaTeX-biblatex-use-Biber` variable.

`LaTeX-biblatex-use-Biber`   [Variable]
> If this boolean variable is set as file local, it tells to AUCTeX whether to use Biber with biblatex. In this case, the autodetection of the biblatex backend will be overridden. You may want to set locally this variable if automatic parsing is not enabled.

After confirming a command to execute, AUCTeX will try to save any buffers related to the document, and check if the document needs to be reformatted. If the variable `TeX-save-query` is non-nil, AUCTeX will query before saving each file. By default AUCTeX will check emacs buffers associated with files in the current directory, in one of the `TeX-macro-private` directories, and in the `TeX-macro-global` directories. You can change this by setting the variable `TeX-check-path`.

`TeX-check-path`   [User Option]
> Directory path to search for dependencies.

> If nil, just check the current file. Used when checking if any files have changed.

4.1.3 Options for TeX Processors

There are some options you can customize affecting which processors are invoked or the way this is done and which output they produce as a result. These options control if DVI or PDF output should be produced, if TeX should be started in interactive or nonstop mode, if source specials or a SyncTeX file should be produced for making inverse and forward search possible or which TeX engine should be used instead of regular TeX, like PDFTeX, Omega or XeTeX.

`TeX-PDF-mode`   [Command]
> (*C-c C-t C-p*) This command toggles the PDF mode of AUCTeX, a buffer-local minor mode which is enabled by default. You can customize `TeX-PDF-mode` to give it a different default or set it as a file local variable on a per-document basis. This option usually results in calling either PDFTeX or ordinary TeX.

`TeX-DVI-via-PDFTeX`   [User Option]
> If this is set, DVI will also be produced by calling PDFTeX, setting `\pdfoutput=0`. This makes it possible to use PDFTeX features like character protrusion even when producing DVI files. Contemporary TeX distributions do this anyway, so that you need not enable the option within AUCTeX.

TeX-interactive-mode   [Command]

    (*C-c C-t C-i*) This command toggles the interactive mode of AUCTeX, a global minor mode. You can customize **TeX-interactive-mode** to give it a different default. In interactive mode, TeX will pause with an error prompt when errors are encountered and wait for the user to type something.

TeX-source-correlate-mode   [Command]

    (*C-c C-t C-s*) Toggles support for forward and inverse search. Forward search refers to jumping to the place in the previewed document corresponding to where point is located in the document source and inverse search to the other way round. See Section 4.2.2 [I/O Correlation], page 55.

    You can permanently activate **TeX-source-correlate-mode** by customizing the variable **TeX-source-correlate-mode**. There is a bunch of customization options for the mode, use *M-x customize-group RET TeX-view RET* to find out more.

    AUCTeX is aware of three different means to do I/O correlation: source specials (only DVI output), the pdfsync LaTeX package (only PDF output) and SyncTeX. The choice between source specials and SyncTeX can be controlled with the variable **TeX-source-correlate-method**.

    Should you use source specials it has to be stressed *very* strongly however, that source specials can cause differences in page breaks and spacing, can seriously interfere with various packages and should thus *never* be used for the final version of a document. In particular, fine-tuning the page breaks should be done with source specials switched off.

AUCTeX also allows you to easily select different TeX engines for processing, either by using the entries in the 'TeXing Options' submenu below the 'Command' menu or by calling the function **TeX-engine-set**. These eventually set the variable **TeX-engine** which you can also modify directly.

TeX-engine   [User Option]

    This variable allows you to choose which TeX engine should be used for typesetting the document, i.e. the executables which will be used when you invoke the 'TeX' or 'LaTeX' commands. The value should be one of the symbols defined in **TeX-engine-alist-builtin** or **TeX-engine-alist**. The symbols 'default', 'xetex', 'luatex' and 'omega' are available from the built-in list.

Note that **TeX-engine** is buffer-local, so setting the variable directly or via the above mentioned menu or function will not take effect in other buffers. If you want to activate an engine for all AUCTeX modes, set **TeX-engine** in your init file, e.g. by using *M-x customize-variable <RET>*. If you want to activate it for a certain AUCTeX mode only, set the variable in the respective mode hook. If you want to activate it for certain files, set it through file variables (see Section "File Variables" in *The Emacs Editor*).

Should you need to change the executable names related to the different engine settings, there are some variables you can tweak. Those are **TeX-command**, **LaTeX-command**, **TeX-Omega-command**, **LaTeX-Omega-command**, **ConTeXt-engine** and **ConTeXt-Omega-engine**. The rest of the executables is defined directly in **TeX-engine-alist-builtin**. If you want to override an entry from that, add an entry to **TeX-engine-alist** that starts with the same symbol as that the entry in the built-in list and specify the executables you want to use instead. You can also add entries to `TeX-engine-alist` in order to add support for engines not covered per default.

`TeX-engine-alist`   [User Option]
> Alist of TeX engines and associated commands. Each entry is a list with a maximum of five elements. The first element is a symbol used to identify the engine. The second is a string describing the engine. The third is the command to be used for plain TeX. The fourth is the command to be used for LaTeX. The fifth is the command to be used for the '`--engine`' parameter of ConTeXt's '`texexec`' program. Each command can either be a variable or a string. An empty string or nil means there is no command available.

As shown above, AUCTeX handles in a special way most of the main options that can be given to the TeX processors. When you need to pass to the TeX processor arbitrary options not handled by AUCTeX, you can use the file local variable `TeX-command-extra-options`.

`TeX-command-extra-options`   [User Option]
> String with the extra options to be given to the TeX processor. For example, if you need to enable the shell escape feature to compile a document, add the following line to the list of local variables of the source file:
>
>   %%% TeX-command-extra-options: "-shell-escape"
>
> By default this option is not safe as a file-local variable because a specially crafted document compiled with shell escape enabled can be used for malicious purposes.

You can customize AUCTeX to show the processor output as it is produced.

`TeX-show-compilation`   [User Option]
> If non-nil, the output of TeX compilation is shown in another window.

4.2 Viewing the Formatted Output

AUCTeX allows you to start external programs for previewing the formatted output of your document.

4.2.1 Starting Viewers

Viewers are normally invoked by pressing *C-c C-c* once the document is formatted, which will propose the View command, or by activating the respective entry in the Command menu. Alternatively you can type *C-c C-v* which calls the function `TeX-view`.

`TeX-view`   [Command]
> (*C-c C-v*) Start a viewer without confirmation. The viewer is started either on a region or the master file, depending on the last command issued. This is especially useful for jumping to the location corresponding to point in the viewer when using `TeX-source-correlate-mode`.

AUCTeX will try to guess which type of viewer (DVI, PostScript or PDF) has to be used and what options are to be passed over to it. This decision is based on the output files present in the working directory as well as the class and style options used in the document.

For example, if there is a DVI file in your working directory, a DVI viewer will be invoked. In case of a PDF file it will be a PDF viewer. If you specified a special paper format like 'a5paper' or use the 'landscape' option, this will be passed to the viewer by the appropriate options. Especially some DVI viewers depend on this kind of information in order to display your document correctly. In case you are using 'pstricks' or 'psfrag' in your document, a DVI viewer cannot display the contents correctly and a PostScript viewer will be invoked instead.

The association between the tests for the conditions mentioned above and the viewers is made in the variable TeX-view-program-selection. Therefore this variable is the starting point for customization if you want to use other viewers than the ones suggested by default.

TeX-view-program-selection   [User Option]
    This is a list of predicates and viewers which is evaluated from front to back in order to find out which viewer to call under the given conditions. In the first element of each list item you can reference one or more predicates defined in TeX-view-predicate-list or TeX-view-predicate-list-builtin. In the second element you can reference a viewer defined in TeX-view-program-list or TeX-view-program-list-builtin. The viewer of the first item with a positively evaluated predicate is selected.

So TeX-view-program-selection only contains references to the actual implementations of predicates and viewer commands respectively which can be found elsewhere. AUCTEX comes with a set of preconfigured predicates and viewer commands which are stored in the variables TeX-view-predicate-list-builtin and TeX-view-program-list-builtin respectively. If you are not satisfied with those and want to overwrite one of them or add your own definitions, you can do so via the variables TeX-view-predicate-list and TeX-view-program-list.

TeX-view-predicate-list   [User Option]
    This is a list of predicates for viewer selection and invocation. The first element of each list item is a symbol and the second element a Lisp form to be evaluated. The form should return nil if the predicate is not fulfilled.

    A built-in predicate from TeX-view-predicate-list-builtin can be overwritten by defining a new predicate with the same symbol.

TeX-view-program-list   [User Option]
    This is a list of viewer specifications each consisting of a symbolic name and either a command line or a function to be invoked when the viewer is called. If a command line is used, parts of it can be conditionalized by prefixing them with predicates from TeX-view-predicate-list or TeX-view-predicate-list-builtin. (See the doc string for the exact format to use.) The command line can also contain placeholders as defined in TeX-expand-list which are expanded before the viewer is called.

    A built-in viewer spec from TeX-view-program-list-builtin can be overwritten by defining a new viewer spec with the same name.

Note that the viewer selection and invocation as described above will only work if certain default settings in AUCTEX are intact. For one, the whole viewer selection machinery will only be triggered if the '%V' expander in TeX-expand-list is unchanged. So if you have trouble with the viewer invocation you might check if there is an older customization of the variable in place. In addition, the use of a function in `TeX-view-program-list` only works if the View command in `TeX-command-list` makes use of the hook `TeX-run-discard-or-function`.

Note also that the implementation described above replaces an older one which was less flexible. This old implementation works with the variables `TeX-output-view-style` and `TeX-view-style` which are used to associate file types and style options with viewers. If desired you can reactivate it by using the placeholder '`%vv`' for the View command in `TeX-command-list`. Note however, that it is bound to be removed from AUCTEX once the new implementation proved to be satisfactory. For the time being, find a short description of the mentioned customization options below.

`TeX-output-view-style`   [User Option]
> List of output file extensions, style options and view options. Each item of the list consists of three elements. If the first element (a regular expression) matches the output file extension, and the second element (a regular expression) matches the name of one of the style options, any occurrence of the string `%V` in a command in `TeX-command-list` will be replaced with the third element.

`TeX-view-style`   [User Option]
> List of style options and view options. This is the predecessor of `TeX-output-view-style` which does not provide the possibility to specify output file extensions. It is used as a fallback in case none of the alternatives specified in `TeX-output-view-style` match. In case none of the entries in `TeX-view-style` match either, no suggestion for a viewer is made.

4.2.2 Forward and Inverse Search

Forward and inverse search refer to the correlation between the document source in the editor and the typeset document in the viewer. Forward search allows you to jump to the place in the previewed document corresponding to a certain line in the document source and inverse search vice versa.

AUCTEX supports three methods for forward and inverse search: source specials (only DVI output), the pdfsync LaTeX package (only PDF output) and SyncTeX (any type of output). If you want to make use of forward and inverse searching with source specials or SyncTeX, switch on `TeX-source-correlate-mode`. See Section 4.1.3 [Processor Options], page 51, on how to do that. The use of the pdfsync package is detected automatically if document parsing is enabled. Customize the variable `TeX-source-correlate-method` to select the method to use.

`TeX-source-correlate-method`   [User Option]
> Method to use for enabling forward and inverse search. This can be '`source-specials`' if source specials should be used, '`synctex`' if SyncTeX should be used, or '`auto`' if AUCTEX should decide.

> When the variable is set to '`auto`', AUCTEX will always use SyncTeX if your `latex` processor supports it, source specials otherwise. You must make sure your viewer supports the same method.

> It is also possible to specify a different method depending on the output, either DVI or PDF, by setting the variable to an alist of the kind

```
((dvi . <source-specials or synctex>)
 (pdf . <source-specials or synctex>))
```

in which the CDR of each entry is a symbol specifying the method to be used in the corresponding mode. The default value of the variable is

```
((dvi . source-specials)
 (pdf . synctex))
```

which is compatible with the majority of viewers.

Forward search happens automatically upon calling the viewer, e.g. by typing *C-c C-v* (`TeX-view`). This will open the viewer or bring it to front and display the output page corresponding to the position of point in the source file. AUCTEX will automatically pass the necessary command line options to the viewer for this to happen.

Upon opening the viewer you will be asked if you want to start a server process (Gnuserv or Emacs server) which is necessary for inverse search. This happens only if there is no server running already. You can customize the variable `TeX-source-correlate-start-server` to inhibit the question and always or never start the server respectively.

`TeX-source-correlate-start-server`   [User Option]
    If `TeX-source-correlate-mode` is active and a viewer is invoked, the default behavior is to ask if a server process should be started. Set this variable to `t` if the question should be inhibited and the server should always be started. Set it to `nil` if the server should never be started. Inverse search will not be available in the latter case.

Inverse search, i.e. jumping to the part of your document source in Emacs corresponding to a certain position in the viewer, is triggered from the viewer, typically by a mouse click. Refer to the documentation of your viewer to find out how it has to be configured and what you have to do exactly. In xdvi you normally have to use *C-down-mouse-1*.

4.3 Catching the errors

Once you've formatted your document you may 'debug' it, i.e. browse through the errors (La)TEX reported.

`TeX-next-error` *arg reparse*   [Command]
    (*C-c `*) Go to the next error reported by TEX. The view will be split in two, with the cursor placed as close as possible to the error in the top view. In the bottom view, the error message will be displayed along with some explanatory text.

    An optional numeric *arg*, positive or negative, specifies how many error messages to move. A negative *arg* means to move back to previous error messages, see also `TeX-previous-error`.

    The optional *reparse* argument makes AUCTEX reparse the error message buffer and start the debugging from the first error. This can also be achieved by calling the function with a prefix argument (*C-u*).

`TeX-previous-error` *arg*   [Command]
    (*M-g p*) Go to the previous error reported by TEX. An optional numeric *arg* specifies how many error messages to move backward. This is like calling `TeX-next-error` with a negative argument.

The command `TeX-previous-error` works only if AUCTeX can parse the whole TeX log buffer. This is controlled by the `TeX-parse-all-errors` variable.

`TeX-parse-all-errors`   [User Option]
> If t, AUCTeX automatically parses the whole output log buffer right after running a TeX command, in order to collect all warnings and errors. This makes it possible to navigate back and forth between the error messages using `TeX-next-error` and `TeX-previous-error`. This is the default. If nil, AUCTeX does not parse the whole output log buffer and `TeX-previous-error` cannot be used.

Normally AUCTeX will only report real errors, but you may as well ask it to report 'bad boxes' and warnings as well.

`TeX-toggle-debug-bad-boxes`   [Command]
> (`C-c C-t C-b`) Toggle whether AUCTeX should stop at bad boxes (i.e. overfull and underfull boxes) as well as normal errors.

`TeX-toggle-debug-warnings`   [Command]
> (`C-c C-t C-w`) Toggle whether AUCTeX should stop at warnings as well as normal errors.

As default, AUCTeX will display a special help buffer containing the error reported by TeX along with the documentation. There is however an 'expert' option, which allows you to display the real TeX output.

`TeX-display-help`   [User Option]
> If t AUCTeX will automatically display a help text whenever an error is encountered using `TeX-next-error` (`C-c '`). If nil a terse information about the error is displayed in the echo area. If `expert` AUCTeX will display the output buffer with the raw TeX output.

When the option `TeX-parse-all-errors` is non-nil, you will be also able to open an overview of all errors and warnings reported by the TeX compiler. This feature requires `tabulated-list-mode`, shipped with GNU Emacs 24 or later.

`TeX-error-overview`   [Command]
> Show an overview of the errors and warnings occurred in the last TeX run.
>
> In this window you can visit the error on which point is on by pressing `RET`, and visit the next or previous issue by pressing `n` or `p` respectively. A prefix argument to these keys specifies how many errors to move forward or backward. You can visit an error also by clicking on its message. Press `q` to quit the overview.

`TeX-error-overview-open-after-TeX-run`   [User Option]
> When this boolean variable is non-nil, the error overview will be automatically opened after running TeX if there are errors or warnings to show.

The error overview is opened in a new window of the current frame by default, but you can change this behavior by customizing the option `TeX-error-overview-setup`.

TeX-error-overview-setup [User Option]
> Controls the frame setup of the error overview. The possible value is: `separate-frame`; with a nil value the current frame is used instead.
>
> The parameters of the separate frame can be set with the `TeX-error-overview-frame-parameters` option.
>
> If the display does not support multi frame, the current frame will be used regardless of the value of this variable.

4.4 Checking for problems

Running TeX or LaTeX will only find regular errors in the document, not examples of bad style. Furthermore, description of the errors may often be confusing. The utilities `lacheck` and `chktex` can be used to find style errors, such as forgetting to escape the space after an abbreviation or using '...' instead of '\ldots' and other similar problems. You start `lacheck` with *C-c C-c Check RET* and `chktex` with *C-c C-c ChkTeX RET*. The result will be a list of errors in the '*compilation*' buffer. You can go through the errors with *C-x `* (`next-error`, see Section "Compilation" in *The Emacs Editor*), which will move point to the location of the next error.

Each of the two utilities will find some errors the other doesn't, but `chktex` is more configurable, allowing you to create your own errors. You may need to install the programs before using them. You can get `lacheck` from `<URL:ftp://ftp.ctan.org/tex-archive/support/lacheck/>` and `chktex` from `<URL:ftp://ftp.ctan.org/tex-archive/support/chktex/>`.

4.5 Controlling the output

A number of commands are available for controlling the output of an application running under AUCTeX

TeX-kill-job [Command]
> (*C-c C-k*) Kill currently running external application. This may be either of TeX, LaTeX, previewer, BibTeX, etc.

TeX-recenter-output-buffer [Command]
> (*C-c C-l*) Recenter the output buffer so that the bottom line is visible.

TeX-home-buffer [Command]
> (*C-c ^*) Go to the 'master' file in the document associated with the current buffer, or if already there, to the file where the current process was started.

4.6 Cleaning intermediate and output files

TeX-clean [Command]
> Remove generated intermediate files. In case a prefix argument is given, remove output files as well.
>
> Canonical access to the function is provided by the 'Clean' and 'Clean All' entries in `TeX-command-list`, invokable with *C-c C-c* or the Command menu.

The patterns governing which files to remove can be adapted separately for each AUCTEX   mode   by   means of the variables `plain-TeX-clean-intermediate-suffixes`, `plain-TeX-clean-output-suffixes`, `LaTeX-clean-intermediate-suffixes`, `LaTeX-clean-output-suffixes`, `docTeX-clean-intermediate-suffixes`, `docTeX-clean-output-suffixes`, `Texinfo-clean-intermediate-suffixes`, `Texinfo-clean-output-suffixes`, `ConTeXt-clean-intermediate-suffixes` and `ConTeXt-clean-output-suffixes`.

`TeX-clean-confirm`   [User Option]

Control if deletion of intermediate and output files has to be confirmed before it is actually done. If non-nil, ask before deleting files.

4.7 Documentation about macros and packages

`TeX-doc`   [Command]

(`C-c ?`) Get documentation about macros, packages or TEX & Co. in general. The function will prompt for the name of a command or manual, providing a list of available keywords for completion. If point is on a command or word with available documentation, this will be suggested as default.

In case no documentation could be found, a prompt for querying the '`texdoc`' program is shown, should the latter be available.

The command can be invoked by the key binding mentioned above as well as the '`Find Documentation...`' entry in the mode menu.

5 Customization and Extension

5.1 Modes and Hooks

AUCTeX supports a wide variety of derivatives and extensions of TeX. Besides plain TeX those are LaTeX, AMS-TeX, ConTeXt, Texinfo and docTeX. For each of them there is a separate major mode in AUCTeX and each major mode runs `text-mode-hook`, `TeX-mode-hook` as well as a hook special to the mode in this order. The following table provides an overview of the respective mode functions and hooks.

Type	Mode function	Hook
Plain TeX	`plain-TeX-mode`	`plain-TeX-mode-hook`
LaTeX	`LaTeX-mode`	`LaTeX-mode-hook`
AMS-TeX	`ams-tex-mode`	`AmS-TeX-mode-hook`
ConTeXt	`ConTeXt-mode`	`ConTeXt-mode-hook`
Texinfo	`Texinfo-mode`	`Texinfo-mode-hook`
DocTeX	`docTeX-mode`	`docTeX-mode-hook`

If you need to make a customization via a hook which is only relevant for one of the modes listed above, put it into the respective mode hook, if it is relevant for any AUCTeX mode, add it to `TeX-mode-hook` and if it is relevant for all text modes, append it to `text-mode-hook`.

5.2 Multifile Documents

You may wish to spread a document over many files (as you are likely to do if there are multiple authors, or if you have not yet discovered the power of the outline commands (see Section 3.3 [Outline], page 47)). This can be done by having a "master" file in which you include the various files with the TeX macro '`\input`' or the LaTeX macro '`\include`'. These files may also include other files themselves. However, to format the document you must run the commands on the top level master file.

When you, for example, ask AUCTeX to run a command on the master file, it has no way of knowing the name of the master file. By default, it will assume that the current file is the master file. If you insert the following in your `.emacs` file AUCTeX will use a more advanced algorithm.

```
(setq-default TeX-master nil) ; Query for master file.
```

If AUCTeX finds the line indicating the end of the header in a master file (`TeX-header-end`), it can figure out for itself that this is a master file. Otherwise, it will ask for the name of the master file associated with the buffer. To avoid asking you again, AUCTeX will automatically insert the name of the master file as a file variable (see Section "File Variables" in *The Emacs Editor*). You can also insert the file variable yourself, by putting the following text at the end of your files.

```
%%% Local Variables:
%%% TeX-master: "master"
%%% End:
```

You should always set this variable to the name of the top level document. If you always use the same name for your top level documents, you can set `TeX-master` in your `.emacs` file.

```
(setq-default TeX-master "master") ; All master files called "master".
```

TeX-master   [User Option]

> The master file associated with the current buffer. If the file being edited is actually included from another file, then you can tell AUCTeX the name of the master file by setting this variable. If there are multiple levels of nesting, specify the top level file.
>
> If this variable is `nil`, AUCTeX will query you for the name.
>
> If the variable is `t`, then AUCTeX will assume the file is a master file itself.
>
> If the variable is `shared`, then AUCTeX will query for the name, but will not change the file.

TeX-one-master   [User Option]

> Regular expression matching ordinary TeX files.
>
> You should set this variable to match the name of all files, for which it is a good idea to append a `TeX-master` file variable entry automatically. When AUCTeX adds the name of the master file as a file variable, it does not need to ask next time you edit the file.
>
> If you dislike AUCTeX automatically modifying your files, you can set this variable to '`"<none>"`'. By default, AUCTeX will modify any file with an extension of '`.tex`'.

TeX-master-file-ask   [Command]

> (`C-c _`) Query for the name of a master file and add the respective File Variables (see Section "File Variables" in *The Emacs Editor*) to the file for setting this variable permanently.
>
> AUCTeX will not ask for a master file when it encounters existing files. This function shall give you the possibility to insert the variable manually.

AUCTeX keeps track of macros, environments, labels, and style files that are used in a given document. For this to work with multifile documents, AUCTeX has to have a place to put the information about the files in the document. This is done by having an `auto` subdirectory placed in the directory where your document is located. Each time you save a file, AUCTeX will write information about the file into the `auto` directory. When you load a file, AUCTeX will read the information in the `auto` directory about the file you loaded *and the master file specified by* `TeX-master`. Since the master file (perhaps indirectly) includes all other files in the document, AUCTeX will get information from all files in the document. This means that you will get from each file, for example, completion for all labels defined anywhere in the document.

AUCTeX will create the `auto` directory automatically if `TeX-auto-save` is non-nil. Without it, the files in the document will not know anything about each other, except for the name of the master file. See Section 5.5.3 [Automatic Local], page 69.

TeX-save-document   [Command]

> (`C-c C-d`) Save all buffers known to belong to the current document.

`TeX-save-query`   [User Option]

> If non-nil, then query the user before saving each file with `TeX-save-document`.

5.3 Automatic Parsing of TeX Files

AUCTeX depends heavily on being able to extract information from the buffers by parsing them. Since parsing the buffer can be somewhat slow, the parsing is initially disabled. You are encouraged to enable them by adding the following lines to your .emacs file.

```
(setq TeX-parse-self t) ; Enable parse on load.
(setq TeX-auto-save t) ; Enable parse on save.
```

The latter command will make AUCTeX store the parsed information in an `auto` sub-directory in the directory each time the TeX files are stored, see Section 5.5.3 [Automatic Local], page 69. If AUCTeX finds the pre-parsed information when loading a file, it will not need to reparse the buffer. The information in the `auto` directory is also useful for multifile documents, see Section 5.2 [Multifile], page 60, since it allows each file to access the parsed information from all the other files in the document. This is done by first reading the information from the master file, and then recursively the information from each file stored in the master file.

The variables can also be done on a per file basis, by changing the file local variables.

```
%%% Local Variables:
%%% TeX-parse-self: t
%%% TeX-auto-save: t
%%% End:
```

Even when you have disabled the automatic parsing, you can force the generation of style information by pressing `C-c C-n`. This is often the best choice, as you will be able to decide when it is necessary to reparse the file.

`TeX-parse-self`   [User Option]

> Parse file after loading it if no style hook is found for it.

`TeX-auto-save`   [User Option]

> Automatically save style information when saving the buffer.

`TeX-normal-mode arg`   [Command]

> (`C-c C-n`) Remove all information about this buffer, and apply the style hooks again. Save buffer first including style information. With optional argument, also reload the style hooks.

When AUCTeX saves your buffer, it can optionally convert all tabs in your buffer into spaces. Tabs confuse AUCTeX's error message parsing and so should generally be avoided. However, tabs are significant in some environments, and so by default AUCTeX does not remove them. To convert tabs to spaces when saving a buffer, insert the following in your .emacs file:

```
(setq TeX-auto-untabify t)
```

`TeX-auto-untabify`   [User Option]

> Automatically remove all tabs from a file before saving it.

Instead of disabling the parsing entirely, you can also speed it significantly up by limiting the information it will search for (and store) when parsing the buffer. You can do this by setting the default values for the buffer local variables `TeX-auto-regexp-list` and `TeX-auto-parse-length` in your `.emacs` file.

```
;; Only parse LaTeX class and package information.
(setq-default TeX-auto-regexp-list 'LaTeX-auto-minimal-regexp-list)
;; The class and package information is usually near the beginning.
(setq-default TeX-auto-parse-length 2000)
```

This example will speed the parsing up significantly, but AUCTEX will no longer be able to provide completion for labels, macros, environments, or bibitems specified in the document, nor will it know what files belong to the document.

These variables can also be specified on a per file basis, by changing the file local variables.

```
%%% Local Variables:
%%% TeX-auto-regexp-list: TeX-auto-full-regexp-list
%%% TeX-auto-parse-length: 999999
%%% End:
```

TeX-auto-regexp-list [User Option]
List of regular expressions used for parsing the current file.

TeX-auto-parse-length [User Option]
Maximal length of TEX file that will be parsed.

The pre-specified lists of regexps are defined below. You can use these before loading AUCTEX by quoting them, as in the example above.

TeX-auto-empty-regexp-list [Constant]
Parse nothing

LaTeX-auto-minimal-regexp-list [Constant]
Only parse LATEX class and packages.

LaTeX-auto-label-regexp-list [Constant]
Only parse LATEX labels.

LaTeX-auto-index-regexp-list [Constant]
Only parse LATEX index and glossary entries.

LaTeX-auto-class-regexp-list [Constant]
Only parse macros in LATEX classes and packages.

LaTeX-auto-pagestyle-regexp-list [Constant]
Only parse LATEX pagestyles.

LaTeX-auto-counter-regexp-list [Constant]
Only parse LATEX counters.

LaTeX-auto-length-regexp-list [Constant]
Only parse LATEX lengths.

`LaTeX-auto-savebox-regexp-list`   [Constant]
> Only parse LaTeX saveboxes.

`LaTeX-auto-regexp-list`   [Constant]
> Parse common LaTeX commands.

`plain-TeX-auto-regexp-list`   [Constant]
> Parse common plain TeX commands.

`TeX-auto-full-regexp-list`   [Constant]
> Parse all TeX and LaTeX commands that AUCTeX can use.

5.4 Language Support

TeX and Emacs are usable for European (Latin, Cyrillic, Greek) based languages. Some LaTeX and EmacsLisp packages are available for easy typesetting and editing documents in European languages.

For CJK (Chinese, Japanese, and Korean) languages, Emacs or XEmacs with MULE (MULtilingual Enhancement to GNU Emacs) support is required. MULE is part of Emacs by default since Emacs 20. XEmacs has to be configured with the '`--with-mule`' option. Special versions of TeX are needed for CJK languages: CTeX and ChinaTeX for Chinese, ASCII pTeX and NTT jTeX for Japanese, HLaTeX and kTeX for Korean. The CJK-LaTeX package is required for supporting multiple CJK scripts within a single document.

Note that Unicode is not fully supported in Emacs 21 and XEmacs 21. CJK characters are not usable. Please use the MULE-UCS EmacsLisp package or Emacs 22 (not released yet) if you need CJK.

5.4.1 Using AUCTeX with European Languages

5.4.1.1 Typing and Displaying Non-ASCII Characters

First you will need a way to write non-ASCII characters. You can either use macros, or teach TeX about the ISO character sets. I prefer the latter, it has the advantage that the usual standard emacs word movement and case change commands will work.

With LaTeX2e, just add '`\usepackage[latin1]{inputenc}`'. Other languages than Western European ones will probably have other encoding needs.

To be able to display non-ASCII characters you will need an appropriate font and a version of GNU Emacs capable of displaying 8-bit characters (e.g. Emacs 21). The manner in which this is supported differs between Emacsen, so you need to take a look at your respective documentation.

A compromise is to use an European character set when editing the file, and convert to TeX macros when reading and writing the files.

`iso-cvt.el`
> Much like `iso-tex.el` but is bundled with Emacs 19.23 and later.

`x-compose.el`
> Similar package bundled with new versions of XEmacs.

`X-Symbol` a much more complete package for both Emacs and XEmacs that can also handle a lot of mathematical characters and input methods.

5.4.1.2 Style Files for Different Languages

AUCTEX supports style files for several languages. Each style file may modify AUCTEX
to better support the language, and will run a language specific hook that will allow
you to for example change ispell dictionary, or run code to change the keyboard remap-
ping. The following will for example choose a Danish dictionary for documents including
'\usepackage[danish]{babel}'. This requires parsing to be enabled, see Section 5.3 [Pars-
ing Files], page 62.

```
(add-hook 'TeX-language-dk-hook
    (lambda () (ispell-change-dictionary "danish")))
```

The following style files are recognized:

bulgarian

Runs style hook `TeX-language-bg-hook`. Gives '"' word syntax, makes the "
key insert a literal '"'. Typing " twice will insert insert '"‘' or '"’' depending
on context. Typing - twice will insert '"=', three times '--'.

czech Runs style hook `TeX-language-cz-hook`. Pressing " will insert '\uv{' and '}'
depending on context.

danish Runs style hook `TeX-language-dk-hook`. Pressing " will insert '"‘' and '"’'
depending on context. Typing - twice will insert '"=', i.e. a hyphen string
allowing hyphenation in the composing words.

dutch Runs style hook `TeX-language-nl-hook`.

english Runs style hook `TeX-language-en-hook`.

frenchb
francais Runs style hook `TeX-language-fr-hook`. Pressing " will insert '\\og' and
'\\fg' depending on context. Note that the language name for customizing
`TeX-quote-language-alist` is 'french'.

german
ngerman Runs style hook `TeX-language-de-hook`. Gives '"' word syntax, makes the "
key insert a literal '"'. Pressing the key twice will give you opening or closing
German quotes ('"‘' or '"’'). Typing - twice will insert '"=', three times '--'.

icelandic

Runs style hook `TeX-language-is-hook`. Gives '"' word syntax, makes the "
key insert a literal '"'. Typing " twice will insert insert '"‘' or '"’' depending
on context. Typing - twice will insert '"=', three times '--'.

italian Runs style hook `TeX-language-it-hook`. Pressing " will insert '"<' and '">'
depending on context.

polish Runs style hook `TeX-language-pl-hook`. Gives '"' word syntax and makes the
" key insert a literal '"'. Pressing " twice will insert '"‘' or '"’' depending on
context.

polski Runs style hook `TeX-language-pl-hook`. Makes the " key insert a literal '"'.
Pressing " twice will insert ',,' or '’’' depending on context.

slovak   Runs style hook `TeX-language-sk-hook`. Pressing " will insert '\uv{' and '}' depending on context.

swedish   Runs style hook `TeX-language-sv-hook`. Pressing " will insert '' ''. Typing - twice will insert '"=', three times '--'.

Replacement of language-specific hyphen strings like '"=' with dashes does not require to type - three times in a row. You can put point after the hypen string anytime and trigger the replacement by typing -.

In case you are not satisfied with the suggested behavior of quote and hyphen insertion you can change it by customizing the variables `TeX-quote-language-alist` and `LaTeX-babel-hyphen-language-alist` respectively.

`TeX-quote-language-alist`   [User Option]

Used for overriding the default language-specific quote insertion behavior. This is an alist where each element is a list consisting of four items. The first item is the name of the language in concern as a string. See the list of supported languages above. The second item is the opening quotation mark. The third item is the closing quotation mark. Opening and closing quotation marks can be specified directly as strings or as functions returning a string. The fourth item is a boolean controlling quote insertion. It should be non-nil if if the special quotes should only be used after inserting a literal '"' character first, i.e. on second key press.

`LaTeX-babel-hyphen-language-alist`   [User Option]

Used for overriding the behavior of hyphen insertion for specific languages. Every element in this alist is a list of three items. The first item should specify the affected language as a string. The second item denotes the hyphen string to be used as a string. The third item, a boolean, controls the behavior of hyphen insertion and should be non-nil if the special hyphen should be inserted after inserting a literal '-' character, i.e. on second key press.

The defaults of hyphen insertion are defined by the variables `LaTeX-babel-hyphen` and `LaTeX-babel-hyphen-after-hyphen` respectively.

`LaTeX-babel-hyphen`   [User Option]

String to be used when typing -. This usually is a hyphen alternative or hyphenation aid provided by 'babel' and the related language style files, like '"=', '"~' or '"-'.

Set it to an empty string or nil in order to disable language-specific hyphen insertion.

`LaTeX-babel-hyphen-after-hyphen`   [User Option]

Control insertion of hyphen strings. If non-nil insert normal hyphen on first key press and swap it with the language-specific hyphen string specified in the variable `LaTeX-babel-hyphen` on second key press. If nil do it the other way round.

5.4.2 Using AUCTeX with Japanese TeX

To write Japanese text with AUCTeX, you need to have versions of TeX and Emacs that support Japanese. There exist at least two variants of TeX for Japanese text (NTT jTeX and ASCII pTeX). AUCTeX can be used with MULE (MULtilingual Enhancement to GNU Emacs) supported Emacsen.

To use the Japanese TeX variants, simply activate `japanese-plain-tex-mode` or `japanese-latex-mode` and everything should work. If not, send mail to Masayuki Ataka '`<ataka@milk.freemail.ne.jp>`', who kindly donated the code for supporting Japanese in AUCTeX. None of the primary AUCTeX maintainers understand Japanese, so they cannot help you.

If you usually use AUCTeX in Japanese, setting the following variables is useful.

`TeX-default-mode`   [User Option]

> Mode to enter for a new file when it cannott be determined whether the file is plain TeX or LaTeX or what.
>
> If you want to enter Japanese LaTeX mode whenever this may happen, set the variable like this:
>
> > `(setq TeX-default-mode 'japanese-latex-mode)`

`japanese-TeX-command-default`   [User Option]

> The default command for `TeX-command` in Japanese TeX mode.
>
> The default value is '`"pTeX"`'.

`japanese-LaTeX-command-default`   [User Option]

> The default command for `TeX-command` in Japanese LaTeX mode.
>
> The default value is '`"LaTeX"`'.

`japanese-LaTeX-default-style`   [User Option]

> The default style/class when creating a new Japanese LaTeX document.
>
> The default value is '`"jarticle"`'.

See `tex-jp.el` for more information.

5.5 Automatic Customization

Since AUCTeX is so highly customizable, it makes sense that it is able to customize itself. The automatic customization consists of scanning TeX files and extracting symbols, environments, and things like that.

The automatic customization is done on three different levels. The global level is the level shared by all users at your site, and consists of scanning the standard TeX style files, and any extra styles added locally for all users on the site. The private level deals with those style files you have written for your own use, and use in different documents. You may have a `~/lib/TeX/` directory where you store useful style files for your own use. The local level is for a specific directory, and deals with writing customization for the files for your normal TeX documents.

If compared with the environment variable `TEXINPUTS`, the global level corresponds to the directories built into TeX. The private level corresponds to the directories you add yourself, except for ., which is the local level.

By default AUCTeX will search for customization files in all the global, private, and local style directories, but you can also set the path directly. This is useful if you for example want to add another person's style hooks to your path. Please note that all matching files found in `TeX-style-path` are loaded, and all hooks defined in the files will be executed.

`TeX-style-path`   [User Option]
> List of directories to search for AUCTEX style files. Each must end with a slash.

By default, when AUCTEX searches a directory for files, it will recursively search through subdirectories.

`TeX-file-recurse`   [User Option]
> Whether to search TEX directories recursively: nil means do not recurse, a positive integer means go that far deep in the directory hierarchy, t means recurse indefinitely.

By default, AUCTEX will ignore files named ., .., `SCCS`, `RCS`, and `CVS`.

`TeX-ignore-file`   [User Option]
> Regular expression matching file names to ignore.

> These files or directories will not be considered when searching for TEX files in a directory.

5.5.1 Automatic Customization for the Site

Assuming that the automatic customization at the global level was done when AUCTEX was installed, your choice is now: will you use it? If you use it, you will benefit by having access to all the symbols and environments available for completion purposes. The drawback is slower load time when you edit a new file and perhaps too many confusing symbols when you try to do a completion.

You can disable the automatic generated global style hooks by setting the variable `TeX-auto-global` to nil.

`TeX-macro-global`   [User Option]
> Directories containing the site's TEX style files.

`TeX-style-global`   [User Option]
> Directory containing hand generated TEX information. Must end with a slash.

> These correspond to TEX macros shared by all users of a site.

`TeX-auto-global`   [User Option]
> Directory containing automatically generated information.

> For storing automatic extracted information about the TEX macros shared by all users of a site.

5.5.2 Automatic Customization for a User

You should specify where you store your private TEX macros, so AUCTEX can extract their information. The extracted information will go to the directories listed in `TeX-auto-private`

Use `M-x TeX-auto-generate RET` to extract the information.

`TeX-macro-private`   [User Option]
> Directories where you store your personal TEX macros. The value defaults to the directories listed in the 'TEXINPUTS' and 'BIBINPUTS' environment variables or to the respective directories in `$TEXMFHOME` if no results can be obtained from the environment variables.

`TeX-auto-private` [User Option]

> List of directories containing automatically generated AUCTEX style files. These correspond to the personal TEX macros.

`TeX-auto-generate` *TEX AUTO* [Command]

> (*M-x TeX-auto-generate RET*) Generate style hook for *TEX* and store it in *AUTO*. If *TEX* is a directory, generate style hooks for all files in the directory.

`TeX-style-private` [User Option]

> List of directories containing hand generated AUCTEX style files. These correspond to the personal TEX macros.

5.5.3 Automatic Customization for a Directory

AUCTEX can update the style information about a file each time you save it, and it will do this if the directory `TeX-auto-local` exist. `TeX-auto-local` is by default set to '`"auto"`', so simply creating an `auto` directory will enable automatic saving of style information.

The advantage of doing this is that macros, labels, etc. defined in any file in a multifile document will be known in all the files in the document. The disadvantage is that saving will be slower. To disable, set `TeX-auto-local` to nil.

`TeX-style-local` [User Option]

> Directory containing hand generated TEX information. Must end with a slash.
>
> These correspond to TEX macros found in the current directory.

`TeX-auto-local` [User Option]

> Directory containing automatically generated TEX information. Must end with a slash.
>
> These correspond to TEX macros found in the current directory.

5.6 Writing Your Own Style Support

See Section 5.5 [Automatic], page 67, for a discussion about automatically generated global, private, and local style files. The hand generated style files are equivalent, except that they by default are found in `style` directories instead of `auto` directories.

If you write some useful support for a public TEX style file, please send it to us.

5.6.1 A Simple Style File

Here is a simple example of a style file.

```
;;; book.el - Special code for book style.

(TeX-add-style-hook
 "book"
 (lambda ()
   (LaTeX-largest-level-set "chapter"))
 LaTeX-dialect)
```

The example is from the AUCTEX sources and is loaded for any LaTeX document using the book document class (or style before LaTeX2e). The file specifies that the largest kind of section in such a document is chapter. The interesting thing to notice is that the style file defines an (anonymous) function, and adds it to the list of loaded style hooks by calling `TeX-add-style-hook`.

The first time the user indirectly tries to access some style-specific information, such as the largest sectioning command available, the style hooks for all files directly or indirectly read by the current document are executed. The actual files will only be evaluated once, but the hooks will be called for each buffer using the style file.

Note that the basename of the style file and the name of the style hook should usually be identical.

TeX-add-style-hook *style hook* **&optional** *dialect-expr*   [Function]
> Add *hook* to the list of functions to run when we use the TeX file *style* and the current dialect is one in the set derived from *dialect-expr*. When *dialect-expr* is omitted, then *hook* is allowed to be run whatever the current dialect is.
>
> *dialect-expr* may be one of:
>
> - A symbol indicating a singleton containing one basic TeX dialect, this symbol shall be selected among:
>
>   `:latex`   For all files in LaTeX mode, or any mode derived thereof
>
>   `:bibtex`   For all files in BibTeX mode, or any mode derived thereof
>
>   `:texinfo`   For all files in Texinfo mode.
>
> - A logical expression like:
>
>   **(or** *dialect-expression1* ... *dialect-expression_n*)
>   > For union of the sets of dialects corresponding to *dialect-expression1* through *dialect-expression_n*
>
>   **(and** *dialect-expression1* ... *dialect-expression_n*)
>   > For intersection of the sets of dialects corresponding to *dialect-expression1* through *dialect-expression_n*
>
>   **(nor** *dialect-expression1* ... *dialect-expression_n*)
>   > For complement of the union sets of dialects corresponding to *dialect-expression1* through *dialect-expression_n* relatively to the set of all supported dialects
>
>   **(not** *dialect-expr*)
>   > For complement set of dialect corresponding to *dialect-expr* relatively to the set of all supported dialects

In case of adding a style hook for LaTeX, when calling function `TeX-add-style-hook` it is thought more futureproof for argument *dialect-expr* to pass constant `LaTeX-dialect` currently defined to `:latex`, rather than passing `:latex` directly.

LaTeX-dialect   [Constant]
> Default dialect for use with function `TeX-add-style-hook` for argument *dialect-expr* when the hook is to be run only on LaTeX file, or any mode derived thereof.

5.6.2 Adding Support for Macros

The most common thing to define in a style hook is new symbols (TeX macros). Most likely along with a description of the arguments to the function, since the symbol itself can be defined automatically.

Here are a few examples from `latex.el`.

```
(TeX-add-style-hook
 "latex"
 (lambda ()
   (TeX-add-symbols
    '("arabic" TeX-arg-counter)
    '("label" TeX-arg-define-label)
    '("ref" TeX-arg-ref)
    '("newcommand" TeX-arg-define-macro [ "Number of arguments" ] t)
    '("newtheorem" TeX-arg-define-environment
      [ TeX-arg-environment "Numbered like" ]
      t [ TeX-arg-counter "Within counter" ]))))
```

`TeX-add-symbols` *symbol* ...   [Function]
> Add each *symbol* to the list of known symbols.

Each argument to `TeX-add-symbols` is a list describing one symbol. The head of the list is the name of the symbol, the remaining elements describe each argument.

If there are no additional elements, the symbol will be inserted with point inside braces. Otherwise, each argument of this function should match an argument of the TeX macro. What is done depends on the argument type.

If a macro is defined multiple times, AUCTeX will chose the one with the longest definition (i.e. the one with the most arguments).

Thus, to overwrite

```
'("tref" 1) ; one argument
```

you can specify

```
'("tref" TeX-arg-ref ignore) ; two arguments
```

`ignore` is a function that does not do anything, so when you insert a 'tref' you will be prompted for a label and no more.

You can use the following types of specifiers for arguments:

string
> Use the string as a prompt to prompt for the argument.

number
> Insert that many braces, leave point inside the first. 0 and -1 are special. 0 means that no braces are inserted. -1 means that braces are inserted around the macro and an active region (e.g. '{\tiny foo}'). If there is no active region, no braces are inserted.

nil
> Insert empty braces.

t
> Insert empty braces, leave point between the braces.

other symbols
> Call the symbol as a function. You can define your own hook, or use one of the predefined argument hooks.

list   If the car is a string, insert it as a prompt and the next element as initial input. Otherwise, call the car of the list with the remaining elements as arguments.

vector   Optional argument. If it has more than one element, parse it as a list, otherwise parse the only element as above. Use square brackets instead of curly braces, and is not inserted on empty user input.

A lot of argument hooks have already been defined. The first argument to all hooks is a flag indicating if it is an optional argument. It is up to the hook to determine what to do with the remaining arguments, if any. Typically the next argument is used to overwrite the default prompt.

`TeX-arg-conditional`
> Implements if EXPR THEN ELSE. If EXPR evaluates to true, parse THEN as an argument list, else parse ELSE as an argument list.

`TeX-arg-literal`
> Insert its arguments into the buffer. Used for specifying extra syntax for a macro.

`TeX-arg-free`
> Parse its arguments but use no braces when they are inserted.

`TeX-arg-eval`
> Evaluate arguments and insert the result in the buffer.

`TeX-arg-label`
> Prompt for a label completing with known labels. If RefTeX is active, prompt for the reference format.

`TeX-arg-ref`
> Prompt for a label completing with known labels. If RefTeX is active, do not prompt for the reference format. Usually, reference macros should use this function instead of `TeX-arg-label`.

`TeX-arg-index-tag`
> Prompt for an index tag. This is the name of an index, not the entry.

`TeX-arg-index`
> Prompt for an index entry completing with known entries.

`TeX-arg-length`
> Prompt for a LaTeX length completing with known lengths.

`TeX-arg-macro`
> Prompt for a TeX macro with completion.

`TeX-arg-date`
> Prompt for a date, defaulting to the current date. The format of the date is specified by the `TeX-date-format` option. If you want to change the format when the 'babel' package is loaded with a specific language, set `TeX-date-format` inside the appropriate language hook, for details see Section 5.4.1 [European], page 64.

`TeX-arg-version`
>   Prompt for the version of a file, using as initial input the current date.

`TeX-arg-environment`
>   Prompt for a LaTeX environment with completion.

`TeX-arg-cite`
>   Prompt for a BibTeX citation. If the variable `TeX-arg-cite-note-p` is non-nil, ask also for optional note in citations.

`TeX-arg-counter`
>   Prompt for a LaTeX counter completing with known counters.

`TeX-arg-savebox`
>   Prompt for a LaTeX savebox completing with known saveboxes.

`TeX-arg-file`
>   Prompt for a filename in the current directory, and use it without the extension.

`TeX-arg-file-name`
>   Prompt for a filename and use as initial input the name of the file being visited in the current buffer, with extension.

`TeX-arg-file-name-sans-extension`
>   Prompt for a filename and use as initial input the name of the file being visited in the current buffer, without extension.

`TeX-arg-input-file`
>   Prompt for the name of an input file in TeX's search path, and use it without the extension. Run the style hooks for the file. (Note that the behavior (type of prompt and inserted file name) of the function can be controlled by the variable `TeX-arg-input-file-search`.)

`TeX-arg-define-label`
>   Prompt for a label completing with known labels. Add label to list of defined labels.

`TeX-arg-define-length`
>   Prompt for a LaTeX length completing with known lengths. Add length to list of defined lengths.

`TeX-arg-define-macro`
>   Prompt for a TeX macro with completion. Add macro to list of defined macros.

`TeX-arg-define-environment`
>   Prompt for a LaTeX environment with completion. Add environment to list of defined environments.

`TeX-arg-define-cite`
>   Prompt for a BibTeX citation.

`TeX-arg-define-counter`
>   Prompt for a LaTeX counter.

`TeX-arg-define-savebox`
>   Prompt for a LaTeX savebox.

TeX-arg-document

> Prompt for a LaTeX document class, using `LaTeX-default-style` as default value and `LaTeX-default-options` as default list of options. If the variable `TeX-arg-input-file-search` is t, you will be able to complete with all LaTeX classes available on your system, otherwise classes listed in the variable `LaTeX-style-list` will be used for completion. It is also provided completion for options of many common classes.

LaTeX-arg-usepackage

> Prompt for LaTeX packages. If the variable `TeX-arg-input-file-search` is t, you will be able to complete with all LaTeX packages available on your system. It is also provided completion for options of many common packages.

TeX-arg-bibstyle

> Prompt for a BibTeX style file completing with all style available on your system.

TeX-arg-bibliography

> Prompt for BibTeX database files completing with all databases available on your system.

TeX-arg-corner

> Prompt for a LaTeX side or corner position with completion.

TeX-arg-lr

> Prompt for a LaTeX side with completion.

TeX-arg-tb

> Prompt for a LaTeX side with completion.

TeX-arg-pagestyle

> Prompt for a LaTeX pagestyle with completion.

TeX-arg-verb

> Prompt for delimiter and text.

TeX-arg-pair

> Insert a pair of numbers, use arguments for prompt. The numbers are surrounded by parentheses and separated with a comma.

TeX-arg-size

> Insert width and height as a pair. No arguments.

TeX-arg-coordinate

> Insert x and y coordinates as a pair. No arguments.

LaTeX-arg-author

> Prompt for document author, using `LaTeX-default-author` as initial input.

TeX-read-key-val

> Prompt for a key=value list of options and return them.

TeX-arg-key-val

> Prompt for a key=value list of options and insert it as a TeX macro argument.

If you add new hooks, you can assume that point is placed directly after the previous argument, or after the macro name if this is the first argument. Please leave point located after the argument you are inserting. If you want point to be located somewhere else after all hooks have been processed, set the value of `exit-mark`. It will point nowhere, until the argument hook sets it.

Some packages provide macros that are rarely useful to non-expert users. Those should be marked as expert macros using `TeX-declare-expert-macros`.

TeX-declare-expert-macros *style macros...* [Function]
Declare MACROS as expert macros of STYLE.

Expert macros are completed depending on 'TeX-complete-expert-commands'.

5.6.3 Adding Support for Environments

Adding support for environments is very much like adding support for TeX macros, except that each environment normally only takes one argument, an environment hook. The example is again a short version of `latex.el`.

```
(TeX-add-style-hook
 "latex"
 (lambda ()
   (LaTeX-add-environments
    '("document" LaTeX-env-document)
    '("enumerate" LaTeX-env-item)
    '("itemize" LaTeX-env-item)
    '("list" LaTeX-env-list))))
```

It is completely up to the environment hook to insert the environment, but the function `LaTeX-insert-environment` may be of some help. The hook will be called with the name of the environment as its first argument, and extra arguments can be provided by adding them to a list after the hook.

For simple environments with arguments, for example defined with '\newenvironment', you can make AUCTeX prompt for the arguments by giving the prompt strings in the call to `LaTeX-add-environments`. The fact that an argument is optional can be indicated by wrapping the prompt string in a vector.

For example, if you have defined a `loop` environment with the three arguments *from*, *to*, and *step*, you can add support for them in a style file.

```
%% loop.sty

\newenvironment{loop}[3]{...}{...}
;; loop.el

(TeX-add-style-hook
 "loop"
 (lambda ()
   (LaTeX-add-environments
    '("loop" "From" "To" "Step"))))
```

If an environment is defined multiple times, AUCTEX will choose the one with the longest definition. Thus, if you have an enumerate style file, and want it to replace the standard LATEX enumerate hook above, you could define an `enumerate.el` file as follows, and place it in the appropriate style directory.

```
(TeX-add-style-hook
 "latex"
 (lambda ()
   (LaTeX-add-environments
    '("enumerate" LaTeX-env-enumerate foo))))
```

```
(defun LaTeX-env-enumerate (environment &optional ignore) ...)
```

The symbol `foo` will be passed to `LaTeX-env-enumerate` as the second argument, but since we only added it to overwrite the definition in `latex.el` it is just ignored.

LaTeX-add-environments *env* ...   [Function]
Add each *env* to list of loaded environments.

LaTeX-insert-environment *env* [*extra*]   [Function]
Insert environment of type *env*, with optional argument *extra*.

Following is a list of available hooks for **LaTeX-add-environments**:

LaTeX-env-item
Insert the given environment and the first item.

LaTeX-env-figure
Insert the given figure-like environment with a caption and a label.

LaTeX-env-array
Insert the given array-like environment with position and column specifications.

LaTeX-env-label
Insert the given environment with a label.

LaTeX-env-list
Insert the given list-like environment, a specifier for the label and the first item.

LaTeX-env-minipage
Insert the given minipage-like environment with position and width specifications.

LaTeX-env-tabular*
Insert the given tabular*-like environment with width, position and column specifications.

LaTeX-env-picture
Insert the given environment with width and height specifications.

LaTeX-env-bib
Insert the given environment with a label for a bibitem.

LaTeX-env-contents
Insert the given environment with a filename as its argument.

`LaTeX-env-args`

> Insert the given environment with arguments. You can use this as a hook in case you want to specify multiple complex arguments just like in elements of `TeX-add-symbols`. This is most useful if the specification of arguments to be prompted for with strings and strings wrapped in a vector as described above is too limited.
>
> Here is an example from `listings.el` which calls a function with one argument in order to prompt for a key=value list to be inserted as an optional argument of the 'lstlisting' environment:

```
(LaTeX-add-environments
 '("lstlisting" LaTeX-env-args
   [TeX-arg-key-val LaTeX-listings-key-val-options]))
```

Some packages provide environments that are rarely useful to non-expert users. Those should be marked as expert environments using `LaTeX-declare-expert-environments`.

`LaTeX-declare-expert-environments` *style ENVIRONMENTS...*   [Function]

> Declare ENVIRONMENTS as expert environments of STYLE.
>
> Expert environments are completed depending on 'TeX-complete-expert-commands'.

5.6.4 Adding Other Information

You can also specify bibliographical databases and labels in the style file. This is probably of little use, since this information will usually be automatically generated from the TeX file anyway.

`LaTeX-add-bibliographies` *bibliography* ...   [Function]

> Add each *bibliography* to list of loaded bibliographies.

`LaTeX-add-labels` *label* ...   [Function]

> Add each *label* to the list of known labels.

5.6.5 Automatic Extraction of New Things

The automatic TeX information extractor works by searching for regular expressions in the TeX files, and storing the matched information. You can add support for new constructs to the parser, something that is needed when you add new commands to define symbols.

For example, in the file `macro.tex` I define the following macro.

```
\newcommand{\newmacro}[5]{%
\def#1{#3\index{#4@#5~cite{#4}}\nocite{#4}}%
\def#2{#5\index{#4@#5~cite{#4}}\nocite{#4}}%
}
```

AUCTeX will automatically figure out that 'newmacro' is a macro that takes five arguments. However, it is not smart enough to automatically see that each time we use the macro, two new macros are defined. We can specify this information in a style hook file.

```
;;; macro.el --- Special code for my own macro file.

;;; Code:
```

```
(defvar TeX-newmacro-regexp
  '("\\\\newmacro{\\\\\\\\([a-zA-Z]+\\)}{\\\\\\\\([a-zA-Z]+\\)}"
    (1 2) TeX-auto-multi)
  "Matches \newmacro definitions.")

(defvar TeX-auto-multi nil
  "Temporary for parsing \\newmacro definitions.")

(defun TeX-macro-cleanup ()
  "Move symbols from 'TeX-auto-multi' to 'TeX-auto-symbol'."
  (mapcar (lambda (list)
    (mapcar (lambda (symbol)
      (setq TeX-auto-symbol
    (cons symbol TeX-auto-symbol)))
    list))
  TeX-auto-multi))

(defun TeX-macro-prepare ()
  "Clear 'Tex-auto-multi' before use."
  (setq TeX-auto-multi nil))

(add-hook 'TeX-auto-prepare-hook 'TeX-macro-prepare)
(add-hook 'TeX-auto-cleanup-hook 'TeX-macro-cleanup)

(TeX-add-style-hook
 "macro"
 (lambda ()
   (TeX-auto-add-regexp TeX-newmacro-regexp)
   (TeX-add-symbols '("newmacro"
     TeX-arg-macro
     (TeX-arg-macro "Capitalized macro: \\")
     t
     "BibTeX entry: "
     nil))))
```

```
;;; macro.el ends here
```

When this file is first loaded, it adds a new entry to **TeX-newmacro-regexp**, and defines a function to be called before the parsing starts, and one to be called after the parsing is done. It also declares a variable to contain the data collected during parsing. Finally, it adds a style hook which describes the 'newmacro' macro, as we have seen it before.

So the general strategy is: Add a new entry to **TeX-newmacro-regexp**. Declare a variable to contain intermediate data during parsing. Add hook to be called before and after parsing. In this case, the hook before parsing just initializes the variable, and the hook after parsing collects the data from the variable, and adds them to the list of symbols found.

TeX-auto-regexp-list [Variable]

List of regular expressions matching TeX macro definitions.

The list has the following format ((REGEXP MATCH TABLE) ...), that is, each entry is a list with three elements.

REGEXP. Regular expression matching the macro we want to parse.

MATCH. A number or list of numbers, each representing one parenthesized subexpression matched by REGEXP.

TABLE. The symbol table to store the data. This can be a function, in which case the function is called with the argument MATCH. Use `TeX-match-buffer` to get match data. If it is not a function, it is presumed to be the name of a variable containing a list of match data. The matched data (a string if MATCH is a number, a list of strings if MATCH is a list of numbers) is put in front of the table.

TeX-auto-prepare-hook *nil* [Variable]
    List of functions to be called before parsing a TeX file.

TeX-auto-cleanup-hook *nil* [Variable]
    List of functions to be called after parsing a TeX file.

Appendix A Copying, Changes, Development, FAQ, Texinfo Mode

A.1 Copying this Manual

The full license text can be read here:

A.1.1 GNU Free Documentation License

Version 1.3, 3 November 2008

Copyright © 2000, 2001, 2002, 2007, 2008 Free Software Foundation, Inc. `http://fsf.org/`

Everyone is permitted to copy and distribute verbatim copies of this license document, but changing it is not allowed.

0. PREAMBLE

The purpose of this License is to make a manual, textbook, or other functional and useful document *free* in the sense of freedom: to assure everyone the effective freedom to copy and redistribute it, with or without modifying it, either commercially or non-commercially. Secondarily, this License preserves for the author and publisher a way to get credit for their work, while not being considered responsible for modifications made by others.

This License is a kind of "copyleft", which means that derivative works of the document must themselves be free in the same sense. It complements the GNU General Public License, which is a copyleft license designed for free software.

We have designed this License in order to use it for manuals for free software, because free software needs free documentation: a free program should come with manuals providing the same freedoms that the software does. But this License is not limited to software manuals; it can be used for any textual work, regardless of subject matter or whether it is published as a printed book. We recommend this License principally for works whose purpose is instruction or reference.

1. APPLICABILITY AND DEFINITIONS

This License applies to any manual or other work, in any medium, that contains a notice placed by the copyright holder saying it can be distributed under the terms of this License. Such a notice grants a world-wide, royalty-free license, unlimited in duration, to use that work under the conditions stated herein. The "Document", below, refers to any such manual or work. Any member of the public is a licensee, and is addressed as "you". You accept the license if you copy, modify or distribute the work in a way requiring permission under copyright law.

A "Modified Version" of the Document means any work containing the Document or a portion of it, either copied verbatim, or with modifications and/or translated into another language.

A "Secondary Section" is a named appendix or a front-matter section of the Document that deals exclusively with the relationship of the publishers or authors of the Document to the Document's overall subject (or to related matters) and contains nothing that could fall directly within that overall subject. (Thus, if the Document is in part a textbook of mathematics, a Secondary Section may not explain any mathematics.) The relationship could be a matter of historical connection with the subject or with related matters, or of legal, commercial, philosophical, ethical or political position regarding them.

The "Invariant Sections" are certain Secondary Sections whose titles are designated, as being those of Invariant Sections, in the notice that says that the Document is released under this License. If a section does not fit the above definition of Secondary then it is not allowed to be designated as Invariant. The Document may contain zero Invariant Sections. If the Document does not identify any Invariant Sections then there are none.

The "Cover Texts" are certain short passages of text that are listed, as Front-Cover Texts or Back-Cover Texts, in the notice that says that the Document is released under this License. A Front-Cover Text may be at most 5 words, and a Back-Cover Text may be at most 25 words.

A "Transparent" copy of the Document means a machine-readable copy, represented in a format whose specification is available to the general public, that is suitable for revising the document straightforwardly with generic text editors or (for images composed of pixels) generic paint programs or (for drawings) some widely available drawing editor, and that is suitable for input to text formatters or for automatic translation to a variety of formats suitable for input to text formatters. A copy made in an otherwise Transparent file format whose markup, or absence of markup, has been arranged to thwart or discourage subsequent modification by readers is not Transparent. An image format is not Transparent if used for any substantial amount of text. A copy that is not "Transparent" is called "Opaque".

Examples of suitable formats for Transparent copies include plain ASCII without markup, Texinfo input format, LaTeX input format, SGML or XML using a publicly available DTD, and standard-conforming simple HTML, PostScript or PDF designed for human modification. Examples of transparent image formats include PNG, XCF and JPG. Opaque formats include proprietary formats that can be read and edited only by proprietary word processors, SGML or XML for which the DTD and/or processing tools are not generally available, and the machine-generated HTML, PostScript or PDF produced by some word processors for output purposes only.

The "Title Page" means, for a printed book, the title page itself, plus such following pages as are needed to hold, legibly, the material this License requires to appear in the title page. For works in formats which do not have any title page as such, "Title Page" means the text near the most prominent appearance of the work's title, preceding the beginning of the body of the text.

The "publisher" means any person or entity that distributes copies of the Document to the public.

A section "Entitled XYZ" means a named subunit of the Document whose title either is precisely XYZ or contains XYZ in parentheses following text that translates XYZ in another language. (Here XYZ stands for a specific section name mentioned below, such as "Acknowledgements", "Dedications", "Endorsements", or "History".) To "Preserve the Title" of such a section when you modify the Document means that it remains a section "Entitled XYZ" according to this definition.

The Document may include Warranty Disclaimers next to the notice which states that this License applies to the Document. These Warranty Disclaimers are considered to be included by reference in this License, but only as regards disclaiming warranties: any other implication that these Warranty Disclaimers may have is void and has no effect on the meaning of this License.

2. VERBATIM COPYING

You may copy and distribute the Document in any medium, either commercially or noncommercially, provided that this License, the copyright notices, and the license notice saying this License applies to the Document are reproduced in all copies, and that you add no other conditions whatsoever to those of this License. You may not use technical measures to obstruct or control the reading or further copying of the copies you make or distribute. However, you may accept compensation in exchange for copies. If you distribute a large enough number of copies you must also follow the conditions in section 3.

You may also lend copies, under the same conditions stated above, and you may publicly display copies.

3. COPYING IN QUANTITY

If you publish printed copies (or copies in media that commonly have printed covers) of the Document, numbering more than 100, and the Document's license notice requires Cover Texts, you must enclose the copies in covers that carry, clearly and legibly, all these Cover Texts: Front-Cover Texts on the front cover, and Back-Cover Texts on the back cover. Both covers must also clearly and legibly identify you as the publisher of these copies. The front cover must present the full title with all words of the title equally prominent and visible. You may add other material on the covers in addition. Copying with changes limited to the covers, as long as they preserve the title of the Document and satisfy these conditions, can be treated as verbatim copying in other respects.

If the required texts for either cover are too voluminous to fit legibly, you should put the first ones listed (as many as fit reasonably) on the actual cover, and continue the rest onto adjacent pages.

If you publish or distribute Opaque copies of the Document numbering more than 100, you must either include a machine-readable Transparent copy along with each Opaque copy, or state in or with each Opaque copy a computer-network location from which the general network-using public has access to download using public-standard network protocols a complete Transparent copy of the Document, free of added material. If you use the latter option, you must take reasonably prudent steps, when you begin distribution of Opaque copies in quantity, to ensure that this Transparent copy will remain thus accessible at the stated location until at least one year after the last time you distribute an Opaque copy (directly or through your agents or retailers) of that edition to the public.

It is requested, but not required, that you contact the authors of the Document well before redistributing any large number of copies, to give them a chance to provide you with an updated version of the Document.

4. MODIFICATIONS

You may copy and distribute a Modified Version of the Document under the conditions of sections 2 and 3 above, provided that you release the Modified Version under precisely this License, with the Modified Version filling the role of the Document, thus licensing distribution and modification of the Modified Version to whoever possesses a copy of it. In addition, you must do these things in the Modified Version:

A. Use in the Title Page (and on the covers, if any) a title distinct from that of the Document, and from those of previous versions (which should, if there were any, be listed in the History section of the Document). You may use the same title as a previous version if the original publisher of that version gives permission.

B. List on the Title Page, as authors, one or more persons or entities responsible for authorship of the modifications in the Modified Version, together with at least five of the principal authors of the Document (all of its principal authors, if it has fewer than five), unless they release you from this requirement.

C. State on the Title page the name of the publisher of the Modified Version, as the publisher.

D. Preserve all the copyright notices of the Document.

E. Add an appropriate copyright notice for your modifications adjacent to the other copyright notices.

F. Include, immediately after the copyright notices, a license notice giving the public permission to use the Modified Version under the terms of this License, in the form shown in the Addendum below.

G. Preserve in that license notice the full lists of Invariant Sections and required Cover Texts given in the Document's license notice.

H. Include an unaltered copy of this License.

I. Preserve the section Entitled "History", Preserve its Title, and add to it an item stating at least the title, year, new authors, and publisher of the Modified Version as given on the Title Page. If there is no section Entitled "History" in the Document, create one stating the title, year, authors, and publisher of the Document as given on its Title Page, then add an item describing the Modified Version as stated in the previous sentence.

J. Preserve the network location, if any, given in the Document for public access to a Transparent copy of the Document, and likewise the network locations given in the Document for previous versions it was based on. These may be placed in the "History" section. You may omit a network location for a work that was published at least four years before the Document itself, or if the original publisher of the version it refers to gives permission.

K. For any section Entitled "Acknowledgements" or "Dedications", Preserve the Title of the section, and preserve in the section all the substance and tone of each of the contributor acknowledgements and/or dedications given therein.

L. Preserve all the Invariant Sections of the Document, unaltered in their text and in their titles. Section numbers or the equivalent are not considered part of the section titles.

M. Delete any section Entitled "Endorsements". Such a section may not be included in the Modified Version.

N. Do not retitle any existing section to be Entitled "Endorsements" or to conflict in title with any Invariant Section.

O. Preserve any Warranty Disclaimers.

If the Modified Version includes new front-matter sections or appendices that qualify as Secondary Sections and contain no material copied from the Document, you may at your option designate some or all of these sections as invariant. To do this, add their titles to the list of Invariant Sections in the Modified Version's license notice. These titles must be distinct from any other section titles.

You may add a section Entitled "Endorsements", provided it contains nothing but endorsements of your Modified Version by various parties—for example, statements of peer review or that the text has been approved by an organization as the authoritative definition of a standard.

You may add a passage of up to five words as a Front-Cover Text, and a passage of up to 25 words as a Back-Cover Text, to the end of the list of Cover Texts in the Modified Version. Only one passage of Front-Cover Text and one of Back-Cover Text may be added by (or through arrangements made by) any one entity. If the Document already includes a cover text for the same cover, previously added by you or by arrangement made by the same entity you are acting on behalf of, you may not add another; but you may replace the old one, on explicit permission from the previous publisher that added the old one.

The author(s) and publisher(s) of the Document do not by this License give permission to use their names for publicity for or to assert or imply endorsement of any Modified Version.

5. COMBINING DOCUMENTS

You may combine the Document with other documents released under this License, under the terms defined in section 4 above for modified versions, provided that you include in the combination all of the Invariant Sections of all of the original documents, unmodified, and list them all as Invariant Sections of your combined work in its license notice, and that you preserve all their Warranty Disclaimers.

The combined work need only contain one copy of this License, and multiple identical Invariant Sections may be replaced with a single copy. If there are multiple Invariant Sections with the same name but different contents, make the title of each such section unique by adding at the end of it, in parentheses, the name of the original author or publisher of that section if known, or else a unique number. Make the same adjustment to the section titles in the list of Invariant Sections in the license notice of the combined work.

In the combination, you must combine any sections Entitled "History" in the various original documents, forming one section Entitled "History"; likewise combine any sections Entitled "Acknowledgements", and any sections Entitled "Dedications". You must delete all sections Entitled "Endorsements."

6. COLLECTIONS OF DOCUMENTS

You may make a collection consisting of the Document and other documents released under this License, and replace the individual copies of this License in the various documents with a single copy that is included in the collection, provided that you follow the rules of this License for verbatim copying of each of the documents in all other respects.

You may extract a single document from such a collection, and distribute it individually under this License, provided you insert a copy of this License into the extracted document, and follow this License in all other respects regarding verbatim copying of that document.

7. AGGREGATION WITH INDEPENDENT WORKS

A compilation of the Document or its derivatives with other separate and independent documents or works, in or on a volume of a storage or distribution medium, is called an "aggregate" if the copyright resulting from the compilation is not used to limit the legal rights of the compilation's users beyond what the individual works permit. When the Document is included in an aggregate, this License does not apply to the other works in the aggregate which are not themselves derivative works of the Document.

If the Cover Text requirement of section 3 is applicable to these copies of the Document, then if the Document is less than one half of the entire aggregate, the Document's Cover Texts may be placed on covers that bracket the Document within the aggregate, or the electronic equivalent of covers if the Document is in electronic form. Otherwise they must appear on printed covers that bracket the whole aggregate.

8. TRANSLATION

Translation is considered a kind of modification, so you may distribute translations of the Document under the terms of section 4. Replacing Invariant Sections with translations requires special permission from their copyright holders, but you may include translations of some or all Invariant Sections in addition to the original versions of these Invariant Sections. You may include a translation of this License, and all the license notices in the Document, and any Warranty Disclaimers, provided that you also include the original English version of this License and the original versions of those notices and disclaimers. In case of a disagreement between the translation and the original version of this License or a notice or disclaimer, the original version will prevail.

If a section in the Document is Entitled "Acknowledgements", "Dedications", or "History", the requirement (section 4) to Preserve its Title (section 1) will typically require changing the actual title.

9. TERMINATION

You may not copy, modify, sublicense, or distribute the Document except as expressly provided under this License. Any attempt otherwise to copy, modify, sublicense, or distribute it is void, and will automatically terminate your rights under this License.

However, if you cease all violation of this License, then your license from a particular copyright holder is reinstated (a) provisionally, unless and until the copyright holder explicitly and finally terminates your license, and (b) permanently, if the copyright holder fails to notify you of the violation by some reasonable means prior to 60 days after the cessation.

Moreover, your license from a particular copyright holder is reinstated permanently if the copyright holder notifies you of the violation by some reasonable means, this is the first time you have received notice of violation of this License (for any work) from that copyright holder, and you cure the violation prior to 30 days after your receipt of the notice.

Termination of your rights under this section does not terminate the licenses of parties who have received copies or rights from you under this License. If your rights have been terminated and not permanently reinstated, receipt of a copy of some or all of the same material does not give you any rights to use it.

10. FUTURE REVISIONS OF THIS LICENSE

The Free Software Foundation may publish new, revised versions of the GNU Free Documentation License from time to time. Such new versions will be similar in spirit to the present version, but may differ in detail to address new problems or concerns. See `http://www.gnu.org/copyleft/`.

Each version of the License is given a distinguishing version number. If the Document specifies that a particular numbered version of this License "or any later version" applies to it, you have the option of following the terms and conditions either of that specified version or of any later version that has been published (not as a draft) by the Free Software Foundation. If the Document does not specify a version number of this License, you may choose any version ever published (not as a draft) by the Free Software Foundation. If the Document specifies that a proxy can decide which future versions of this License can be used, that proxy's public statement of acceptance of a version permanently authorizes you to choose that version for the Document.

11. RELICENSING

"Massive Multiauthor Collaboration Site" (or "MMC Site") means any World Wide Web server that publishes copyrightable works and also provides prominent facilities for anybody to edit those works. A public wiki that anybody can edit is an example of such a server. A "Massive Multiauthor Collaboration" (or "MMC") contained in the site means any set of copyrightable works thus published on the MMC site.

"CC-BY-SA" means the Creative Commons Attribution-Share Alike 3.0 license published by Creative Commons Corporation, a not-for-profit corporation with a principal place of business in San Francisco, California, as well as future copyleft versions of that license published by that same organization.

"Incorporate" means to publish or republish a Document, in whole or in part, as part of another Document.

An MMC is "eligible for relicensing" if it is licensed under this License, and if all works that were first published under this License somewhere other than this MMC, and subsequently incorporated in whole or in part into the MMC, (1) had no cover texts or invariant sections, and (2) were thus incorporated prior to November 1, 2008.

The operator of an MMC Site may republish an MMC contained in the site under CC-BY-SA on the same site at any time before August 1, 2009, provided the MMC is eligible for relicensing.

ADDENDUM: How to use this License for your documents

To use this License in a document you have written, include a copy of the License in the document and put the following copyright and license notices just after the title page:

```
Copyright (C)  year  your name.
Permission is granted to copy, distribute and/or modify this document
under the terms of the GNU Free Documentation License, Version 1.3
or any later version published by the Free Software Foundation;
with no Invariant Sections, no Front-Cover Texts, and no Back-Cover
Texts.  A copy of the license is included in the section entitled ''GNU
Free Documentation License''.
```

If you have Invariant Sections, Front-Cover Texts and Back-Cover Texts, replace the "with...Texts." line with this:

```
with the Invariant Sections being list their titles, with
the Front-Cover Texts being list, and with the Back-Cover Texts
being list.
```

If you have Invariant Sections without Cover Texts, or some other combination of the three, merge those two alternatives to suit the situation.

If your document contains nontrivial examples of program code, we recommend releasing these examples in parallel under your choice of free software license, such as the GNU General Public License, to permit their use in free software.

A.2 Changes and New Features

News in 11.88

- TeX-PDF-mode is now enabled by default.
- Now `TeX-previous-error` works with TeX commands if the new option `TeX-parse-all-errors` is non-nil, which is the default. When this option is non-nil, an overview of errors and warnings reported by the TeX compiler can be opened with *M-x TeX-error-overview RET*. See Section 4.3 [Debugging], page 56, for details.
- Style file authors are encouraged to distinguish common from expert macros and environments, and mark the latter using `TeX-declare-expert-macros` and `LaTeX-declare-expert-environments`.

  Users can then restrict completion using `TeX-complete-expert-commands`.
- Management of LaTeX package options in the parser was improved. You might need to reparse your documents, especially if you loaded the 'babel' package with language options.
- Now you can insert '`$...$`' or '`\(...\)`' by typing a single *$*. To do this, customize the new option '`TeX-electric-math`'. `TeX-math-close-double-dollar` was removed. See Section 2.1 [Quotes], page 20, for details.
- *C-c RET documentclass RET* completes with all available LaTeX classes, if the `TeX-arg-input-file-search` variable is non-nil. Completion for class options of the standard LaTeX classes is provided as well.
- New user options `LaTeX-default-author`, `LaTeX-fontspec-arg-font-search`, `LaTeX-fontspec-font-list-default`, `TeX-date-format`, and `TeX-insert-braces-alist`. A new possible value (`show-all-optional-args`) for `TeX-insert-macro-`

`default-style` was added. The default value of `TeX-source-correlate-method` has been changed.

- 'biblatex' support was greatly expanded. If parsing is enabled, AUCTeX looks at 'backend' option to decide whether to use Biber or BibTeX. The `LaTeX-biblatex-use-Biber` variable was changed to be file local only and is no more customizable.

- With some LaTeX classes, the default environment suggested by `LaTeX-environment` (*C-c C-e*) when the current environment is 'document' was changed. With 'beamer' class the default environment is 'frame', with 'letter' it is 'letter', with 'slides' it is 'slide'.

- Brace pairing feature was enhanced in LaTeX documents. Support for '\bigl', '\Bigl', '\biggl' and '\Biggl', the same as the one for '\left', was added to `TeX-insert-macro`. For example, *C-c RET bigl RET (RET* inserts '\bigl(\bigr)'.

  You can insert brace pair '()', '{}' and '[]' by typing a single left brace if the new user option `LaTeX-electric-left-right-brace` is enabled.

  Macros '\langle', '\lfloor' and '\lceil', which produce the left part of the paired braces, are treated similarly as '(', '{' and '[' during the course of `TeX-insert-macro`. See Section 2.1 [Quotes], page 20, for details.

- Support for dozens of LaTeX packages was added.

- Tabular-like environments (tabular, tabular*, tabularx, tabulary, array, align, ...) are indented in a nicer and more informative way when the column values of a table line are written across multiple lines in the tex file.

- The suitable number of ampersands are inserted when you insert array, tabular and tabular* environments with *C-c C-e*. Similar experience is obtained if you terminate rows in these environments with *C-c LFD*. It supplies line break macro '\\' and inserts the suitable number of ampersands on the next line.

  Similar supports are provided for various amsmath environments.

  See Section 2.4.4 [Tabular-like], page 29, for details.

- Commands for narrowing to a group (`TeX-narrow-to-group`) and to LaTeX environments (`LaTeX-narrow-to-environment`) were added.

- Now arbitrary options can be passed to the TeX processor on a per file basis using the `TeX-command-extra-options` option. See Section 4.1.3 [Processor Options], page 51, for details.

- Now *C-c C-e document RET*, in an empty document, prompts for '\usepackage' macros in addition to '\documentclass'.

- `TeX-add-style-hook` has now a third argument to tell AUCTeX for which dialect (LaTeX, Texinfo or BibTeX) the style hook is registers. Labelling style hook by dialect will avoid applying them not in the right context.

- There have been lots of bug fixes and feature additions.

News since 11.87

- AUCTeX now supports Biber in conjunction with biblatex in addition to BibTeX.

- Each AUCTeX mode now has its own abbrev table. On Emacsen which provide the possibility to inherit abbrevs from other tables, the abbrevs from the Text mode abbrev table are available as well. Newly defined abbrevs are written to the mode-specific tables, though.

- The file 'tex-fptex.el' was removed.

- Forward/backward search for Evince has been improved. If Emacs is compiled with DBUS support and a recent Evince version (3.x) is installed, the communication goes over the desktop bus instead of the command line, resulting in more accurate positioning of point in Emacs and highlighting of the target paragraph in Evince.

- A problem where Ghostscript threw an /invalidfileaccess error when running preview-latex was fixed.

- A lot of smaller fixes and additions have been made.

News in 11.86

- Parsing of LaTeX output was improved. It is now less likely that AUCTeX opens a non-existent file upon calling TeX-next-error; a problem for example encountered when using MiKTeX 2.8. In addition quoted file names as emitted by MiKTeX are now supported.

- A new framework for the definition and selection of viewers was implemented. If you have customizations regarding viewers you will have to redo them in this new framework or reenable the old one. See Section 4.2.1 [Starting Viewers], page 53, for details.

- Comprehensive editing support for PSTricks was added.

- Support for various LaTeX packages was added, e.g. 'tabularx', 'CJK', and 'hyperref'.

- An easy way to switch between TeX engines (PDFTeX, LuaTeX, XeTeX, Omega) was added.

- Support for SyncTeX was added. This involves the command line options for LaTeX and the viewer.

- Folding can now be customized to use macro arguments as replacement text.

- 'preview.sty' now works with XeTeX.

- A lot of smaller and larger bugs have been squashed.

News in 11.85

- Font locking has been improved significantly. It is now less prone to color bleeding which could lead to high resource usage. In addition it now includes information about LaTeX macro syntax and can indicate syntactically incorrect macros in LaTeX mode.

- The license was updated to GPLv3.

- Support for the nomencl, flashcards and comment LaTeX packages as well as the Icelandic language option of babel were added.

- Support for folding of math macros was added.

- Lots of minor bugs in features and documentation fixed.

News in 11.84

- There have been problems with the '-without-texmf-dir' option to 'configure' when the value of '-with-kpathsea-sep' was set or determined for an installation system with a default different from that of the runtime system. `with-kpathsea-sep` has been removed; the setting is now usually determined at runtime.

Due to this and other problems, preview-latex in the released XEmacs package failed under Windows or with anything except recent 21.5 XEmacsen.

- AUCTeX and preview-latex have been changed in order to accommodate file names containing spaces. preview-latex now tolerates bad PostScript code polluting the stack (like some Omega fonts).

- 'preview.sty' had in some cases failed to emit PostScript header specials.

- Support for folding of comments was added.

- The `polish` language option of the babel LaTeX package as well as the polski LaTeX package are now supported. Most notably this means that AUCTeX will help to insert quotation marks as defined by polish.sty ("`..."') and polski.sty (,,...'').

- The TeX tool bar is now available and enabled by default in plain TeX mode. See Section 1.3.2 [Processing Facilities], page 18.

- Bug fix in the display of math subscripts and superscripts.

- Bug fix `TeX-doc` for Emacs 21.

- There has been quite a number of other bug fixes to various features and documentation across the board.

News in 11.83

- The new function `TeX-doc` provides easy access to documentation about commands and packages or information related to TeX and friends in general. See Section 4.7 [Documentation], page 59.

- You can now get rid of generated intermediate and output files by means of the new 'Clean' and 'Clean All' entries in `TeX-command-list` accessible with `C-c C-c` or the Command menu. See Section 4.6 [Cleaning], page 58.

- Support for forward search with PDF files was added. That means you can jump to a place in the output file corresponding to the position in the source file. See Section 4.2 [Viewing], page 53.

  Adding support for this feature required the default value of the variable `TeX-output-view-style` to be changed. Please make sure you either remove any customizations overriding the new default or incorporate the changes into your customizations if you want to use this feature.

- TeX error messages of the `-file-line-error` kind are now understood in AUCTeX and preview-latex (parsers are still separate).

- Bug fix in XyMTeX support.

- The LaTeX tool bar is now enabled by default. See Section 1.3.2 [Processing Facilities], page 18.

News in 11.82

- Support for the MinionPro LaTeX package was added.

- Warnings and underfull/overfull boxes are now being indicated in the echo area after a LaTeX run, if the respective debugging options are activated with `TeX-toggle-debug-warnings` (`C-c C-t C-w`) or `TeX-toggle-debug-bad-boxes` (`C-c C-t C-b`). In this case `TeX-next-error` will find these warnings in addition to normal errors.

  The key binding `C-c C-w` for `TeX-toggle-debug-bad-boxes` (which was renamed from `TeX-toggle-debug-boxes`) now is deprecated.

- AUCTeX now can automatically insert a pair of braces after typing _ or ^ in math constructs if the new variable `TeX-electric-sub-and-superscript` is set to a non-nil value.

- Some language-specific support for French was added. There now is completion support for the commands provided by the 'frenchb' (and 'francais') options of the babel LaTeX package and easier input of French quotation marks (\\og ...\\fg) which can now be inserted by typing ".

- Completion support for options of some LaTeX packages was added.

- Already in version 11.81 the way to activate AUCTeX changed substantially. This should now be done with (load "auctex.el" nil t t) instead of the former (require 'tex-site). Related to this change tex-mik.el does not load tex-site.el anymore. That means if you used only (require 'tex-mik) in order to activate AUCTeX, you have to add (load "auctex.el" nil t t) before the latter statement. See Section 1.2.4 [Loading the package], page 7.

- Handling of verbatim constructs was consolidated across AUCTeX. This resulted in the font-latex-specific variables `font-latex-verb-like-commands`, `font-latex-verbatim-macros`, and `font-latex-verbatim-environments` being removed and the more general variables `LaTeX-verbatim-macros-with-delims`, `LaTeX-verbatim-macros-with-braces`, and `LaTeX-verbatim-environments` being added.

- The output of a BibTeX run is now checked for warnings and errors, which are reported in the echo area.

- The aliases for `font-latex-title-fontify` were removed. Use `font-latex-fontify-sectioning` instead.

- The problem that Japanese macros where broken across lines was fixed.

- Various bug fixes.

News in 11.81

- `LaTeX-mark-section` now marks subsections of a given section as well. The former behavior is available via the prefix argument.

- preview-latex which was previously available separately became a subsystem of AUCTeX. There is no documented provision for building or installing preview-latex separately. It is still possible to use and install AUCTeX without preview-latex, however.

- The installation procedures have been overhauled and now also install startup files as part of the process (those had to be copied manually previously). You are advised to remove previous installations of AUCTeX and preview-latex before starting the installation procedure. A standard installation from an unmodified tarball no longer requires Makeinfo or Perl.

Also note that the way AUCTEX is supposed to be activated changed. Instead of (require 'tex-site) you should now use (load "auctex.el" nil t t). While the former method may still work, the new method has the advantage that you can de-activate a preactivated AUCTEX with the statement (unload-feature 'tex-site) before any of its modes have been used. This may be important especially for site-wide installations.

- Support for the babel LATEX package was added.

- Folding a buffer now ensures that the whole buffer is fontified before the actual folding is carried out. If this results in unbearably long execution times, you can fall back to the old behavior of relying on stealth font locking to do this job in the background by customizing the variable `TeX-fold-force-fontify`.

- Folded content now reveals part of its original text in a tooltip or the echo area when hovering with the mouse pointer over it.

- The language-specific insertion of quotation marks was generalized. The variables `LaTeX-german-open-quote`, `LaTeX-german-close-quote`, `LaTeX-german-quote-after-quote`, `LaTeX-italian-open-quote`, `LaTeX-italian-close-quote`, and `LaTeX-italian-quote-after-quote` are now obsolete. If you are not satisfied with the default settings, you should customize `TeX-quote-language-alist` instead.

- Similar to language-specific quote insertion, AUCTEX now helps you with hyphens in different languages as well. See Section 5.4.1 [European], page 64, for details.

- Fill problems in Japanese text introduced in AUCTEX 11.55 were fixed. AUCTEX tries not to break lines between 1-byte and 2-byte chars. These features will work in Chinese text, too.

- The scaling factor of the fontification of sectioning commands can now be customized using the variable `font-latex-fontify-sectioning`. This variable was previously called `font-latex-title-fontify`; In this release we provide an alias but this will disappear in one of the the next releases. The faces for the sectioning commands are now called `font-latex-sectioning-N-face` ($N=0...5$) instead of `font-latex-title-N-face` ($N=1...4$). Analogously the names of the variables holding the related keyword lists were changed from `font-latex-title-N-keywords` to `font-latex-sectioning-N-keywords`. See Section 3.1 [Font Locking], page 38, for details. Make sure to adjust your customizations.

- Titles in beamer slides marked by the "\frametitle" command are know displayed with the new face `font-latex-slide-title-face`. You can add macros to be highlighted with this face to `font-latex-match-slide-title-keywords`.

- Of course a lot of bugs have been fixed.

News in 11.55

- A bug was fixed which lead to the insertion of trailing whitespace during filling. In particular extra spaces were added to sentence endings at the end of lines. You can make this whitespace visible by setting the variable `show-trailing-whitespace` to t. If you want to delete all trailing whitespace in a buffer, type *M-x delete-trailing-whitespace RET*.

- A bug was fixed which lead to a '`*Compile-Log*`' buffer popping up when the first LaTeX file was loaded in an Emacs session.

- On some systems the presence of an outdated Emacspeak package lead to the error message '`File mode specification error: (error "Variable binding depth exceeds max-specpdl-size")`'. Precautions were added which prevent this error from happening. But nevertheless, it is advised to upgrade or uninstall the outdated Emacspeak package.

- The value of `TeX-macro-global` is not determined during configuration anymore but at load time of AUCTeX. Consequently the associated configuration option '`--with-tex-input-dirs`' was removed.

- Support for the LaTeX Japanese classes '`jsarticle`' and '`jsbook`' was added.

News in 11.54

- The parser (used e.g. for `TeX-auto-generate-global`) was extended to recognize keywords common in LaTeX packages and classes, like "\DeclareRobustCommand" or "\RequirePackage". Additionally a bug was fixed which led to duplicate entries in AUCTeX style files.

- Folding can now be done for paragraphs and regions besides single constructs and the whole buffer. With the new `TeX-fold-dwim` command content can both be hidden and shown with a single key binding. In course of these changes new key bindings for unfolding commands where introduced. The old bindings are still present but will be phased out in future releases.

- Info files of the manual now have a .info extension.

- There is an experimental tool bar support now. It is not activated by default. If you want to use it, add

      (add-hook 'LaTeX-mode-hook 'LaTeX-install-toolbar)

  to your init file.

- The manual now contains a new chapter "Quick Start". It explains the main features and how to use them, and should be enough for a new user to start using AUCTeX.

- A new section "Font Locking" was added to the manual which explains syntax highlighting in AUCTeX and its customization. Together with the sections related to folding and outlining, the section is part of the new chapter "Display".

- Keywords for syntax highlighting of LaTeX constructs to be typeset in bold, italic or typewriter fonts may now be customized. Besides the built-in classes, new keyword classes may be added by customizing the variable '`font-latex-user-keyword-classes`'. The customization options can be found in the customization group '`font-latex-keywords`'.

- Verbatim content is now displayed with the '`fixed-pitch`' face. (GNU Emacs only)

- Syntax highlighting should not spill out of verbatim content anymore. (GNU Emacs only)

- Verbatim commands like '`\verb|...|`' will not be broken anymore during filling.

- You can customize the completion for graphic files with `LaTeX-includegraphics-read-file`.

- Support for the LaTeX packages 'url', 'listings', 'jurabib' and 'csquotes' was added with regard to command completion and syntax highlighting.
- Performance of fontification and filling was improved.
- Insertion of nodes in Texinfo mode now supports completion of existing node names.
- Setting the variable LaTeX-float to nil now means that you will not be prompted for the float position of figures and tables. You can get the old behaviour of nil by setting the variable to "", i.e. an empty string. See also Section 2.4.2 [Floats], page 28.
- The XEmacs-specific bug concerning overlays-at was fixed.
- Lots of bug fixes.

News in 11.53

- The LaTeX math menu can include Unicode characters if your Emacs built supports it. See the variable LaTeX-math-menu-unicode, Section 2.5 [Mathematics], page 30.
- Bug fixes for XEmacs.
- Completion for graphic files in the TeX search path has been added.
- start is used for the viewer for MiKTeX and fpTeX.
- The variable TeX-fold-preserve-comments can now be customized to deactivate folding in comments.

News in 11.52

- Installation and menus under XEmacs work again (maybe for the first time).
- Fontification of subscripts and superscripts is now disabled when the fontification engine is not able to support it properly.
- Bug fixes in the build process.

News in 11.51

- PDFTeX and Source Special support did not work with ConTeXt, this has been fixed. Similar for Source Special support under Windows.
- Omega support has been added.
- Bug fixes in the build process.
- TeX-fold now supports folding of environments in Texinfo mode.

News in 11.50

- The use of source specials when processing or viewing the document can now be controlled with the new TeX-source-specials minor mode which can be toggled via an entry in the Command menu or the key binding C-c C-t C-s. If you have customized the variable TeX-command-list, you have to re-initialize it for this to work. This means to open a customization buffer for the variable by typing M-x customize-variable RET TeX-command-list RET, selecting "Erase Customization" and do your customization again with the new default.

- The content of the command menu now depends on the mode (plain TEX, LATEX, ConTEXt etc.). Any former customization of the variable `TeX-command-list` has to be erased. Otherwise the command menu and the customization will not work correctly.

- Support for hiding and auto-revealing macros, e.g. footnotes or citations, and environments in a buffer was added, Section 3.2 [Folding], page 44.

- You can now control if indentation is done upon typing RET by customizing the variable `TeX-newline-function`, Section 2.9 [Indenting], page 34.

- Limited support for `doc.sty` and `ltxdoc.cls` ('dtx' files) was added. The new docTEX mode provides functionality for editing documentation parts. This includes formatting (indenting and filling), adding and completion of macros and environments while staying in comments as well as syntax highlighting. (Please note that the mode is not finished yet. For example syntax highlighting does not work yet in XEmacs.)

- For macro completion in docTEX mode the AUCTEX style files `doc.el`, `ltxdoc.el` and `ltx-base.el` were included. The latter provides general support for low-level LATEX macros and may be used with LATEX class and style files as well. It is currently not loaded automatically for those files.

- Support for ConTEXt with a separate ConTEXt mode is now included. Macro definitions for completion are available in Dutch and English.

- The filling and indentation code was overhauled and is now able to format commented parts of the source syntactically correct. Newly available functionality and customization options are explained in the manual.

- Filling and indentation in XEmacs with preview-latex and activated previews lead to the insertion of whitespace before multi-line previews. AUCTEX now contains facilities to prevent this problem.

- If `TeX-master` is set to `t`, AUCTEX will now query for a master file only when a new file is opened. Existing files will be left alone. The new function `TeX-master-file-ask` (bound to `C-c _` is provided for adding the variable manually.

- Sectioning commands are now shown in a larger font on display devices which support such fontification. The variable `font-latex-title-fontify` can be customized to restore the old appearance, i.e. the usage of a different color instead of a change in size.

- Support for `alphanum.sty`, `beamer.cls`, `booktabs.sty`, `captcont.sty`, `emp.sty`, `paralist.sty`, `subfigure.sty` and `units.sty`/`nicefrac.sty` was added. Credits go to the authors mentioned in the respective AUCTEX style files.

- Inserting graphics with `C-c RET \includegraphics RET` was improved. See the variable `LaTeX-includegraphics-options-alist`.

- If `LaTeX-default-position` is `nil`, don't prompt for position arguments in Tabular-like environments, see Section 2.4.4 [Tabular-like], page 29.

- Completion for available packages when using `C-c RET \usepackage RET` was improved on systems using the kpathsea library.

- The commenting functionality was fixed. The separate functions for commenting and uncommenting were unified in one function for paragraphs and regions respectively which do both.

- Syntax highlighting can be customized to fontify quotes delimited by either >>German<< or <<French>> quotation marks by changing the variable `font-latex-quotes`.

- Certain TeX/LaTeX keywords for functions, references, variables and warnings will now be fontified specially. You may add your own keywords by customizing the variables `font-latex-match-function-keywords`, `font-latex-match-reference-keywords`, `font-latex-match-variable-keywords` and `font-latex-match-warning-keywords`.

- If you include the style files `german` or `ngerman` in a document (directly or via the 'babel' package), you should now customize `LaTeX-german-open-quote`, `LaTeX-german-close-quote` and `LaTeX-german-quote-after-quote` instead of `TeX-open-quote`, `TeX-close-quote` and `TeX-quote-after-quote` if you want to influence the type of quote insertion.

- Upon viewing an output file, the right viewer and command line options for it are now determined automatically by looking at the extension of the output file and certain options used in the source file. The behavior can be adapted or extended respectively by customizing the variable `TeX-output-view-style`.

- You can control whether `TeX-insert-macro` (*C-c RET*) ask for all optional arguments by customizing the variable `TeX-insert-macro-default-style`, Section 2.6 [Completion], page 31.

- `TeX-run-discard` is now able to completely detach a process that it started.

- The build process was enhanced and is now based on `autoconf` making installing AUCTeX a mostly automatic process. See Section 1.2 [Installation], page 3 and Section 1.2.7 [Installation under MS Windows], page 10 for details.

News in 11.14

- Many more LaTeX and LaTeX2e commands are supported. Done by Masayuki Ataka <ataka@milk.freemail.ne.jp>

News in 11.12

- Support for the KOMA-Script classes. Contributed by Mark Trettin <Mark.Trettin@gmx.de>.

News in 11.11

- Support for `prosper.sty`, see `http://prosper.sourceforge.net/`. Contributed by Phillip Lord <p.lord@russet.org.uk>.

News in 11.10

- `comment-region` now inserts %% by default. Suggested by "Davide G. M. Salvetti" <salve@debian.org>.

News in 11.06

- You can now switch between using the `font-latex` (all emacsen), the `tex-font` (Emacs 21 only) or no special package for font locking. Customize `TeX-install-font-lock` for this.

News in 11.04

- Now use `-t landscape` by default when landscape option appears. Suggested by Erik Frisk <frisk@isy.liu.se>.

News in 11.03

- Use `tex-fptex.el` for fpTeX support. Contributed by Fabrice Popineau <Fabrice.Popineau@supelec.fr>.

News in 11.02

- New user option `LaTeX-top-caption-list` specifies environments where the caption should go at top. Contributed by ataka@milk.freemail.ne.jp (Masayuki Ataka).
- Allow explicit dimensions in `graphicx.sty`. Contributed by ataka@milk.freemail.ne.jp (Masayuki Ataka).
- Limited support for `verbatim.sty`. Contributed by ataka@milk.freemail.ne.jp (Masayuki Ataka).
- Better support for asmmath items. Patch by ataka@milk.freemail.ne.jp (Masayuki Ataka).
- More accurate error parsing. Added by David Kastrup <David.Kastrup@t-online.de>.

News in 11.01

- Bug fixes.

Older versions

See the file `history.texi` for older changes.

A.3 Future Development

The following sections describe future development of AUCTEX. Besides mid-term goals, bug reports and requests we cannot fix or honor right away are being gathered here. If you have some time for Emacs Lisp hacking, you are encouraged to try to provide a solution to one of the following problems. If you don't know Lisp, you may help us to improve the documentation. It might be a good idea to discuss proposed changes on the mailing list of AUCTEX first.

A.3.1 Mid-term Goals

- Integration of preview-latex into AUCTEX

  As of AUCTEX 11.81 preview-latex is a part of AUCTEX in the sense that the installation routines were merged and preview-latex is being packaged with AUCTEX.

  Further integration will happen at the backend. This involves folding of error parsing and task management of both packages which will ease development efforts and avoid redundant work.

- Error help catalogs

  Currently, the help for errors is more or less hardwired into `tex.el`. For supporting error help in other languages, it would be sensible to instead arrange error messages in language-specific files, make a common info file from all such catalogs in a given language and look the error texts up in an appropriate index. The user would then specify a preference list of languages, and the errors would be looked up in the catalogs in sequence until they were identified.

- Combining 'docTeX' with RefTeX

  Macro cross references should also be usable for document navigation using RefTeX.

A.3.2 Wishlist

- Documentation lookup for macros

  A parser could gather information about which macros are defined in which LaTeX packages and store the information in a hashtable which can be used in a backend for TeX-doc in order to open the matching documentation for a given macro. The information could also be used to insert an appropriate '\usepackage' statement if the user tries to insert a macro for which the respective package has not been requested yet.

- Spell checking of macros

  A special ispell dictionary for macros could be nice to have.

- Improvements to error reporting

  Fringe indicators for errors in the main text would be nice.

- A math entry grid

  A separate frame with a table of math character graphics to click on in order to insert the respective sequence into the buffer (cf. the "grid" of x-symbol).

- Crossreferencing support

  It would be nice if you could index process your favorite collection of .dtx files (such as the LaTeX source), just call a command on arbitrary control sequence, and get either the DVI viewer opened right at the definition of that macro (using Source Specials), or the source code of the .dtx file.

- Better plain TeX support

  For starters, LaTeX-math-mode is not very LaTeX-specific in the first place, and similar holds for indentation and formatting.

- Page count when compiling should (optionally) go to modeline of the window where the compilation command was invoked, instead of the output window. Suggested by Karsten Tinnefeld <tinnefeld@irb.informatik.uni-dortmund.de>.

- Command to insert a macrodefinition in the preamble, without moving point from the current location. Suggested by "Jeffrey C. Ely" <ely@nwu.edu>.

- A database of all commands defined in all stylefiles. When a command or environment gets entered that is provided in one of the styles, insert the appropriate \usepackage in the preamble.

- A way to add and overwrite math mode entries in style files, and to decide where they should be. Suggested by Remo Badii <Remo.Badii@psi.ch>.

- Create template for (first) line of tabular environment.

- I think prompting for the master is the intended behaviour. It corresponds to a 'shared' value for TeX-master.

There should probably be a 'none' value which wouldn't query for the master, but instead disable all features that relies on TeX-master.

This default value for TeX-master could then be controled with mapping based on the extension.

- Suggest 'makeindex' when appropriate.
- Use index files (when available) to speed up *C-c C-m include RET*.
- Option not to calculate very slow completions like for *C-c C-m include RET*.
- Font menu should be created from `TeX-font-list`.
- Installation procedure written purely in emacs lisp.
- Included PostScript files should also be counted as part of the document.
- A nice hierarchical by-topic organization of all officially documented LaTeX macros, available from the menu bar.
- `TeX-command-default` should be set from the master file, if not set locally. Suggested by Peter Whaite '`<peta@cim.mcgill.ca>`'.
- Make AUCTEX work with '`crypt++`'. Suggested by Chris Moore '`<Chris.Moore@src.bae.co.uk>`'.
- Make AUCTEX work with '`longlines`'. This would also apply to preview-latex, though it might make sense to unify error processing before attempting this.
- The '`Spell`' command should apply to all files in a document. Maybe it could try to restrict to files that have been modified since last spell check? Suggested by Ravinder Bhumbla '`<rbhumbla@ucsd.edu>`'.
- Make . check for abbreviations and sentences ending with capital letters.
- Use Emacs 19 minibuffer history to choose between previewers, and other stuff. Suggested by John Interrante '`<interran@uluru.Stanford.EDU>`'.
- Make features.

  A new command `TeX-update` (*C-c C-u*) could be used to create an up-to-date dvi file by repeatedly running BibTEX, MakeIndex and (La)TEX, until an error occurs or we are done.

  An alternative is to have an '`Update`' command that ensures the '`dvi`' file is up to date. This could be called before printing and previewing.

- Documentation of variables that can be set in a style hook.

  We need a list of what can safely be done in an ordinary style hook. You can not set a variable that AUCTEX depends on, unless AUCTEX knows that it has to run the style hooks first.

  Here is the start of such a list.

```
LaTeX-add-environments
TeX-add-symbols
LaTeX-add-labels
LaTeX-add-bibliographies
LaTeX-largest-level
```

- Outline should be (better) supported in TEX mode.

  At least, support headers, trailers, as well as TeX-outline-extra.

- `TeX-header-start` and `TeX-trailer-end`.

  We might want these, just for fun (and outlines)

- Plain TeX and LaTeX specific header and trailer expressions.

  We should have a way to globally specify the default value of the header and trailer regexps.

- Get closer to original `TeX-mode` keybindings.

  A third initialization file (`tex-mode.el`) containing an emulator of the standard `TeX-mode` would help convince some people to change to AUCTeX.

- Use markers in `TeX-error-list` to remember buffer positions in order to be more robust with regard to line numbers and changed files.

- Finish the Texinfo mode. For one thing, many Texinfo mode commands do not accept braces around their arguments.

- Hook up the letter environment with `bbdb.el`.

A.3.3 Bugs

- The style hooks automatically generated by parsing files for `example.dtx`, `example.sty`, `example.drv` and `example.bib` all clash. Bad. Clash with hand-written style hooks should be removed by dialect discrimination — to be checked.

- `C-c '` should always stay in the current window, also when it finds a new file.

- Do not overwrite emacs warnings about existing auto-save files when loading a new file.

- Maybe the regexp for matching a TeX symbol during parsing should be `'"\\\\\\([a-zA-Z]+\\|.\\)"'` — `<thiemann@informatik.uni-tuebingen.de>`' Peter Thiemann.

- AUCTeX should not parse verbatim environments.

- Make `''` check for math context in `LaTeX-math-mode`. and simply self insert if not in a math context.

- Make `TeX-insert-dollar` more robust. Currently it can be fooled by `\mbox`''es and escaped double dollar for example.

- Correct indentation for tabular, tabbing, table, math, and array environments.

- No syntactic font locking of verbatim macros and environments. (XEmacs only)

- Font locking inside of verbatim macros and environments is not inhibited. This may result in syntax highlighting of unbalanced dollar signs and the like spilling out of the verbatim content. (XEmacs only)

- Folding of LaTeX constructs spanning more than one line may result in overfull lines. (XEmacs only)

A.4 Frequently Asked Questions

1. Something is not working correctly. What should I do?

   Well, you might have guessed it, the first place to look is in the available documentation packaged with AUCTeX. This could be the release notes (in the **RELEASE** file) or the news section of the manual in case you are experiencing problems after an upgrade, the

INSTALL file in case you are having problems with the installation, the section about bugs in the manual in case you encountered a bug or the relevant sections in the manual for other related problems.

If this did not help, you can send a bug report to the AUCTeX bug reporting list by using the command *M-x TeX-submit-bug-report RET*. But before you do this, you can try to get more information about the problem at hand which might also help you locate the cause of the error yourself.

First, you can try to generate a so-called backtrace which shows the functions involved in a program error. In order to do this, start Emacs with the command line 'emacs --debug-init' and/or put the line

```
(setq debug-on-error t)
```

as the first line into your init file. XEmacs users might want to add (setq stack-trace-on-error t) as well. After Emacs has started, you can load a file which triggers the error and a new window should pop up showing the backtrace. If you get such a backtrace, please include it in the bug report.

Second, you can try to figure out if something in your personal or site configuration triggers the error by starting Emacs without such customizations. You can do this by invoking Emacs with the command line 'emacs -q -no-site-file -l auctex'. The '-l' option 'auctex.el' which you normally do in your init file. After you have started Emacs like this, you can load the file triggering the error. If everything is working now, you know that you have to search either in the site configuration file or your personal init file for statements related to the problem.

2. What versions of Emacs and XEmacs are supported?

   AUCTeX was tested with Emacs 21 and XEmacs 21.4.15. Older versions may work but are unsupported. Older versions of XEmacs might possibly made to work by updating the xemacs-base package through the XEmacs package system. If you are looking for a recommendation, it would appear that the smoothest working platform on all operating systems at the current point of time would be Emacs 22 or higher.

   Our success with XEmacs has been less than convincing. Code for core functionality like formatting and syntax highlighting tends to be different and often older than even Emacs 21.4, and Unicode support as delivered is problematic at best, missing on Windows. Both AUCTeX and XEmacs developers don't hear much from active users of the combination. Partly for that reason, problems tend to go unnoticed for long amounts of time and are often found, if at all, after releases. No experiences or recommendations can be given for beta or developer versions of XEmacs.

3. What should I do when ./configure does not find programs like latex?

   This is problem often encountered on Windows. Make sure that the PATH environment variable includes the directories containing the relevant programs, as described in Section "Installation under MS Windows" in *the AUCTeX manual.*

4. Why doesn't the completion, style file, or multi-file stuff work?

   It must be enabled first, insert this in your init file:

```
(setq-default TeX-master nil)
(setq TeX-parse-self t)
(setq TeX-auto-save t)
```

Read also the chapters about parsing and multifile documents in the manual.

5. Why doesn't `TeX-save-document` work?

   `TeX-check-path` has to contain `"./"` somewhere.

6. Why is the information in `foo.tex` forgotten when I save `foo.bib`?

   For various reasons, AUCTEX ignores the extension when it stores information about a file, so you should use unique base names for your files. E.g. rename `foo.bib` to `foob.bib`.

7. Why doesn't AUCTEX signal when processing a document is done?

   If the message in the minibuffer stays "Type 'C-c C-l' to display results of compilation.", you probably have a misconfiguration in your init file (`.emacs`, `init.el` or similar). To track this down either search in the '`*Messages*`' buffer for an error message or put (`setq debug-on-error t`) as the first line into your init file, restart Emacs and open a LATEX file. Emacs will complain loudly by opening a debugging buffer as soon as an error occurs. The information in the debugging buffer can help you find the cause of the error in your init file.

8. Why does `TeX-next-error` (`C-c '`) fail?

   When writing the log file, TEX puts information related to a file, including error messages, between a pair of parentheses. AUCTEX determines the file where the error happened by parsing the log file and counting the parentheses. This can fail when there are other, unbalanced parentheses present.

   As a workaround you can activate so-called file:line:error messages for the log file. (Those are are easier to parse, but may lack some details.) Either you do this in the configuration of your TEX system (consult its manual to see where this is) or you add a command line switch to the (la)tex call, e.g. by customizing `LaTeX-command-style` or `TeX-command-list`.

9. What does AUC stand for?

   AUCTEX came into being at Aalborg University in Denmark. Back then the Danish name of the university was Aalborg Universitetscenter; AUC for short.

A.5 Features specific to AUCTEX's Texinfo major mode

AUCTEX includes a major mode for editing Texinfo files. This major mode is not the same mode as the native Texinfo mode (see ⟨undefined⟩ [(texinfo) Texinfo Mode], page ⟨undefined⟩) of Emacs, although they have the same name. However, AUCTEX still relies on a number of functions from the native Texinfo mode.

The following text describes which functionality is offered by AUCTEX and which by the native Texinfo mode. This should enable you to decide when to consult the AUCTEX manual and when the manual of the native mode. And in case you are a seasoned user of the native mode, the information should help you to swiftly get to know the AUCTEX-specific commands.

A.5.1 How AUCTEX and the native mode work together

In a nutshell the split between AUCTEX Texinfo mode, and native Texinfo mode is as follows:

- Most of the editing (environment creation, commenting, font command insertions) and/or processing commands (e.g. compiling or printing) which are available in other AUCTEX modes are also handled by AUCTEX in Texinfo mode.
- Texinfo-related features (e.g. info node linkage or menu creation) rely on the commands provided by the native Texinfo mode. AUCTEX provides the key bindings to reach these functions, keeping the same keys as in native Texinfo whenever possible, or similar ones otherwise.

A.5.2 Where the native mode is superseded

This section is directed to users of the native Texinfo mode switching to AUCTEX. It follows the summary of the native mode (see ⟨undefined⟩ [(texinfo) Texinfo Mode Summary], page ⟨undefined⟩) and lists which of its commands are no longer of use.

Insert commands

In the native Texinfo mode, frequently used Texinfo commands can be inserted with key bindings of the form `C-c C-c k` where *k* differs for each Texinfo command; *c* inserts @code, *d* inserts @dfn, *k* @kbd, etc.

In AUCTEX commands are inserted with the key binding `C-c C-m` instead which prompts for the macro to be inserted. For font selection commands (like @b, @i, or @emph) and a few related ones (like @var, @key or @code) there are bindings which insert the respective macros directly. They have the form `C-c C-f k` or `C-c C-f C-k` and call the function `TeX-font`. Type `C-c C-f RET` to get a list of supported commands.

Note that the prefix argument is not handled the same way by AUCTEX. Note also that the node insertion command from the native mode (`texinfo-insert-@node`) can still accessed from the Texinfo menu in AUCTEX.

Insert braces

In AUCTEX braces can be inserted with the same key binding as in the native Texinfo mode: `C-c {`. But AUCTEX uses its own function for the feature: `TeX-insert-braces`.

Insert environments

The native Texinfo mode does not insert full environments. Instead, it provides the function `texinfo-insert-@end` (mapped to `C-c C-c e`) for closing an open environment with a matching @end statement.

In AUCTEX you can insert full environments, i.e. both the opening and closing statements, with the function `Texinfo-environment` (mapped to `C-c C-e`).

Format info files with makeinfo and TEX

In the native Texinfo mode there are various functions and bindings to format a region or the whole buffer for info or to typeset the respective text. For example, there is `makeinfo-buffer` (mapped to `C-c C-m C-b`) which runs 'makeinfo' on the buffer or there is `texinfo-tex-buffer` (mapped to `C-c C-t C-b`) which runs TEX on the buffer in order to produce a DVI file.

In AUCTEX different commands for formatting or typesetting can be invoked through the function `TeX-command-master` (mapped to `C-c C-c`). After typing `C-c C-c`, you can select the desired command, e.g 'Makeinfo' or 'TeX', through a prompt in the mini buffer. Note that you can make, say 'Makeinfo', the default by adding this statement in your init file:

```
(add-hook 'Texinfo-mode-hook
          (lambda () (setq TeX-command-default "Makeinfo")))
```

Note also that *C-c C-c Makeinfo RET* is not completely functionally equivalent to `makeinfo-buffer` as the latter will display the resulting info file in Emacs, showing the node corresponding to the position in the source file, just after a successful compilation. This is why, while using AUCTeX, invoking `makeinfo-buffer` might still be more convenient.

Note also that in the case of a multifile document, *C-c C-c* in AUCTeX will work on the whole document (provided that the file variable `TeX-master` is set correctly), while `makeinfo-buffer` in the native mode will process only the current buffer, provided at the `@setfilename` statement is provided.

Produce indexes and print

The native Texinfo mode provides the binding *C-c C-t C-i* (`texinfo-texindex`) for producing an index and the bindings *C-c C-t C-p* (`texinfo-tex-print`) and *C-c C-t C-q* (`tex-show-print-queue`) for printing and showing the printer queue. These are superseded by the respective commands available through *C-c C-c* (`TeX-command-master`) in AUCTeX: Index, Print, and Queue.

Kill jobs   The command *C-c C-t C-k* (`tex-kill-job`) in the native mode is superseded by *C-c C-k* (`TeX-kill-job`) in AUCTeX.

A.5.3 Where key bindings are mapped to the native mode

This node follows the native Texinfo mode summary (see ⟨undefined⟩ [(texinfo) Texinfo Mode Summary], page ⟨undefined⟩) and lists only those commands to which AUCTeX provides a keybinding.

Basically all commands of the native mode related to producing menus and interlinking nodes are mapped to same or similar keys in AUCTeX, while a few insertion commands are mapped to AUCTeX-like keys.

@item insertion

The binding *C-c C-c i* for the insertion of `@item` in the native mode is mapped to *M-RET* or *C-c C-j* in AUCTeX, similar to other AUCTeX modes.

@end insertion

The binding *C-c C-c e* for closing a `@foo` command by a corresponding `@end foo` statement in the native mode is mapped to *C-c C-]* in AUCTeX, similar to other AUCTeX modes.

Move out of balanced braces

The binding *C-}* (`up-list`) is available both in the native mode and in AUCTeX. (This is because the command is not implemented in either mode but a native Emacs command.) However, in AUCTeX, you cannot use *C-]* for this, as it is used for `@end` insertion.

Update pointers

> The bindings `C-c C-u C-n` (`texinfo-update-node`) and `C-c C-u C-e` (`texinfo-every-node-update`) from the native mode are available in AUCTEX as well.

Update menus

> The bindings `C-c C-u m` (`texinfo-master-menu`), `C-c C-u C-m` (`texinfo-make-menu`), and `C-c C-u C-a` (`texinfo-all-menus-update`) from the native mode are available in AUCTEX as well. The command `texinfo-start-menu-description`, bound to `C-c C-c C-d` in the native mode, is bound to `C-c C-u C-d` in AUCTEX instead.

A.5.4 Which native mode key bindings are missing

The following commands from the native commands might still be useful when working with AUCTEX, however, they are not accessible with a key binding any longer.

@node insertion

> The node insertion command, mapped to `C-c C-c n` in the native mode, is not mapped to any key in AUCTEX. You can still access it through the Texinfo menu, though. Another alternative is to use the `C-c C-m` binding for macro insertion in AUCTEX.

Show the section structure

> The command `texinfo-show-structure` (`C-c C-s`) from the native mode does not have a key binding in AUCTEX. The binding is used by AUCTEX for sectioning.

Indices

Key Index

Function Index

Variable Index

A

C

D

F

J

L

Concept Index